As the owner of a coaching  Norman's new book, *The Tr* challenging as it lays down a ga for coaching mastery, unlearning matters even more than learning. And, according to Norman, we all have plenty to unlearn – we need to unlearn much of what we took from our parents, our school, our peers, our workplace, our managers, our coaching experience and (wait, what?!) even our coach training!

In pursuit of credibility and depth, perhaps something was lost. The simple power of coaching. This is what Norman calls us to reconnect to if we are to achieve mastery as a coach and to make our coaching truly transformational. In a time when coaching is becoming ever more complex, this is a much-needed book that should sit on every coach's bookshelf (and be read)!

– Nick Bolton, founder & CEO, Animas Centre for Coaching

This book takes the reader on an interesting journey... For me the text really came alive when I experimented by taking one example and using it in a coaching session. Wow! Real movement was generated with my client. I tried this again with a supervision client and again, fabulous movement and reaction emerged.

– Tim Anderson, executive coach, mentor coach

In this thought-provoking book, Clare addresses the need of every coach to rewire the things they have learned through life, love and work, removing those old 'scripts', so that they can become extraordinary coaches. Awareness is the precondition of change and Clare makes us aware of 83 biases which have come at us from all directions, and which will be having an impact on our coaching. Reading this book will shed light on the meaning and importance of your prior learning. And you will see how it might be getting in the way of you being the best coach you can be.

This is a must-read book for every coach who wants to get out of their own way, get out of the way of their clients' new thinking, and move a step further toward becoming a great coach.

– Roger Fielding Coach, mentor coach and course tutor, University of Cambridge

Read this book, read this book, read this book – it will liberate you as a coach, help you see ways you can improve and give you practical tips on what that looks like in practice.
– Nicky Chambers, executive and team coach, mentor coach

Coaches are skilled at helping others shift mindsets. Yet some of my biggest learnings and growth have come when I've shifted my own mindset. Clare's work has helped me develop and grow as a coach, and I will always listen to the wise words she shares around shifting mindsets.
– George Warren, executive coach, mentor coach and faculty member of the Academy of Executive Coaching

I haven't previously come across a book which approaches coaches' self-awareness and skill development in this way. What Clare has done here is to bring together all of her wisdom and experience of applying these new mindsets in a way which is accessible and enlightening; her illustrations and stories resonate strongly. I really do think this book will be a goldmine for coaches
– Siobhain Whitty, coach and mentor coach, associate board director, UK ICF

Clare's approach is transforming my coaching. I'm so excited about the insights and progress my clients are consistently making now!
– Jane Bromley, coach

Wow, this is so refreshing – such an original contribution to a somewhat flooded market. Readable and accessible yet evidence based and highly professional. Clare's writing is suitable for beginners *and* seasoned coaches. I felt invigorated and liberated reading this book because it's given me permission to shake off some of the narrow-minded doctrines that some coaching 'experts' propose.
– Mary Andrews, coaching psychologist

The
Transformational Coach

Free your thinking and
break through to coaching mastery

CLARE NORMAN

The Transformational Coach
ISBN 978-1-912300-82-2
eISBN 978-1-912300-83-9

Published in 2022 by Right Book Press
Updated and reprinted in 2024
Printed in the UK

A CIP record of this book is available from the British Library.

Contents

Foreword 1

Jonathan Passmore, Senior Vice President at CoachHub and Professor of Coaching and Behavioural Change, Henley Business School, UK

We can sometimes think coaching is a strange, complex or unusual process. The development of codes of ethics, professional standards, science, research, coach competencies, digital coaching have all moved our understanding of coaching from the simple to the complex.

However, I believe coaching, at its heart, is something that we as humans do naturally: when we set aside our agenda and think of the needs of others. As humans we probably held coaching conversations 10,000 years ago as hunter-gatherers, when working in small groups. The leader of the group might coach their fellow hunters around the options for setting an animal trap or erecting the family shelter. After all, we know coaching is more effective as a personal learning strategy than a directive style of learning.

In many ways we have lost the simplicity of coaching that the very best coaches are able to capture in their work. While they draw on the science and evidence of three or more decades of research, they maintain ethical standards and draw on professional competencies to optimise their performance: like a Jedi Master, they do not lose themself in the process. Instead, they keep it simple.

A return to the heart of coaching is what we need, and this book encourages us to adopt such a mindset. To unlearn the elements which can get in our way, to stay focused on the client and to stay engaged in the conversation. When our mind wanders to reflect on 'Should I adopt a cognitive behavioural approach, or shall I progress using a transpersonal approach?', already we are lost in the mind of complexity.

Staying close to the client, staying close to what they say, is more likely to yield more positive results.

Of course the journey to mastery is, itself, a tricky one. First, the novice needs to learn the core skills, multiple models and build their own integrated framework of practice. They need to master multiple tools, techniques and approaches. Finally, like the advanced driver, they need to be able to provide the running commentary on what and why they are doing what they are doing to demonstrate their competence.

But once integrated into who they are, they need to finally step away from the noise. To once again return to their authentic self: being wholly in service of their client. Finally, they need to hold the beginner's mind. That once again, they are a novice at the feet of a new master: their client. A client who will continue to teach them. A failure to hold on to the beginner's mind, and instead to assume they are a mastermind of coaching, lays a road to hubris and self-service.

Let's unlearn. Let's sit at the feet of our clients. Let us remember the simplicity of coaching.

Foreword 2

Bob Gerard, Learning Ingenuity Lead, Accenture

Coaching is unnatural! At least for me.

I learned this first-hand, right about 1994. After five years as a stand-up technology trainer, I transferred to our global learning team and began facilitating a programme on Client/Server, the three-week-long boot camp programme for new Andersen Consulting analysts. I expected the programme to be the standard type of learning experience I was used to – namely, that I would stand up and teach them how to do something, and they would practise it.

Instead, the course was more of a goal-based scenario. Our new analysts were meant to use at-hand materials and their own resources to teach themselves how to code, all in service of a fictional client. And instead of teaching them, I was supposed to coach them. Not exactly the same type of coaching that you probably do with the people with whom you partner, but pretty darn close.

The first time I ran the class, the course designer gave me some feedback:

'You're teaching too much. You need to coach them.'

'What does that look like?' I asked. 'What do you mean by "coaching?"'

'You know,' he said. 'Coach them.'

I didn't know. But I eventually found out.

Over the years and through many different learning programmes, I discovered some of what makes a good coach. How to ask good questions to help learners discover their own knowledge, instead of just telling them. How to interrupt people, often people who were older than me and at a higher level in the company, to enable them to think about things a different way. How to give direct, pointed and often uncomfortable feedback at a critical moment.

How to coach them. You know, coach them.

The thing is, these are all behaviours that are unnatural for me. They often fly in the face of who I am. I like being the smartest guy in the room and telling people how to do things. I tend to avoid conflict and keep the peace. I don't like hurting people's feelings, and I know how challenging feedback can sting.

Maybe you're wired in a similar way. Maybe you're not. But I bet that inside of you, somewhere, there are some beliefs you hold, some habits you keep, and some tendencies that you gravitate towards that block you from being the best coach you can be.

In this book, Clare shines a blazing-hot spotlight on all of those. All the idiosyncrasies and the habits and the things you know 'just because'. And then she meticulously shows us how they might hinder our coaching practice and what we can do about it.

You might not see yourself in all these chapters. But if you're like me, you'll resonate with most of them. Some of them you'll read and you'll raise your hand and say, 'Mea culpa! How do I get past this?' Fortunately, Clare is right there to help.

I invite you to grab a journal, a cup of coffee and a cosy blanket and dive right in. Savour these chapters and explore each of them yourself. Ask yourself, 'To what extent is this me? And what do I need to think about doing differently?' Let Clare lead you on a journey to becoming the best coach you can be. She can coach you through it.

You know. Coach you.

Introduction

You must unlearn what you have learned

In the film *The Empire Strikes Back*, Yoda, one of the greatest Jedi Masters from a galaxy far, far away, is Luke Skywalker's teacher. He has many words of wisdom for the young man, as Luke learns the ways of the Force. The pair are in a swamp, with Luke learning to use the Force that's all around him to make stones levitate; but then the robot R2-D2 alerts Luke that his spacecraft is sinking into the mud. Luke thinks it's impossible to retrieve his ship, but Yoda suggests that he's too certain of this, and it is this mindset that will get in his way. Luke must unlearn what he has learned. Yoda wants Luke to question what he has been taught, to untangle himself from societal programming.

Coaches don't need to learn to use the Force, but we do need to unlearn ingrained mindsets and beliefs that get in the way of our being the best coaches we could be. For example, we've learned through years of programming from work and life that finding solutions to intractable problems is valued and appreciated.

But in coaching, this is not our role. Our role is to enable the person we're working with to find and own their own solutions that work in their context, given their personality, values, stakeholders and desires. For some coaches, this mindset shift can be just as difficult as believing you can levitate a spacecraft out of a swamp!

I'm often asked by coaches whether this letting go of finding solutions is possible when the person with whom we are working 'doesn't have the life experience to find their own solutions', as one coach put it. But we need to follow through on the notion that they are what Whitworth et al. (1998) described as 'creative, resourceful and whole'. If we believe in their capacity to think, they will think for themselves. If we believe that they don't have the capacity, they won't!

You may understand the paradigm that people are creative, resourceful and whole at a rational level but if, deep down, you're still stuck in the old mindset, you'll likely fall back into the habits that go with it. As Stephen Covey (1999) says: 'If you want small changes, work on your behaviour; if you want quantum-leap changes, work on your paradigms.' He goes on to say that when you change the way you *see* things (your paradigms, mindsets, beliefs, scripts), it influences what you *do* (your habits, your behaviours, your coaching) and the results you *get*.

Back to Yoda: 'You must unlearn [the paradigms, mindsets, beliefs and scripts that]... you have learned.' I use these terms, *paradigms, mindsets, beliefs* and *scripts*, interchangeably throughout this book: they are the way we *see* the world.

Scripts come from the world of Transactional Analysis. According to Stewart and Joines (1987), a script message is 'a verbal or non-verbal message from the parents [or carers] on the basis of which the child forms conclusions about self, others and the world during the process of script making'. We continue to receive verbal and non-verbal messages from other adults in our lives that shape what we believe, and so how we behave. We also receive strokes ('a unit of recognition', according to Stewart and Joines) that encourage us to repeat those behaviours and embed the beliefs or scripts. As coaches we need to unlearn some of the scripts we have formed, the paradigms we hold on to, the mindsets, the beliefs.

According to David Wilkinson in *The Oxford Review Research-based Guide to Unlearning* (2018), it turns out that there is no such scientifically proven thing as 'unlearning'. However, following Covey's 'See–Do–Get' model, and Wilkinson's suggestions as to what *is* possible in terms of reprogramming what we have learned, my wish is that through this book you might:

➡ change the meaning of your prior learning, paradigms, mindsets, beliefs and scripts, so that you *see* them for what they are – not so useful in coaching
➡ replace your old paradigms with new ones that you *see* as more significant, more useful in coaching

➡ make changes to your habits and behaviours that follow the new paradigm
➡ *get* different results – deeper thinking and forward motion in the people with whom you are partnering.

According to Stewart and Joines (1987), we often need permission to let go of old paradigms, beliefs, mindsets and scripts, so I hereby grant you that permission. My intention is for this book to be full of 'positive, liberating script messages' (Stewart and Joines 1987): that is, messages that enable you to change the meaning of your prior learning and replace it with more useful beliefs and mindsets, which in turn help you to make permanent changes to your coaching habits and behaviours.

You *will* see different results, I promise you. The people with whom you're partnering will experience more transformation than you ever thought possible. Isn't that what we all wish for as a result of our coaching?

Who am I to give you that permission? Someone who has studied other coaches for years, and seen the difference that a shift in the coach's mindset can make to the thinking process of the person with whom they're working – so I hope you will take that permission as my gift to you.

My approach to coaching

I practise non-directive coaching. Non-directive means that I don't:

➡ provide answers
➡ lead people to answers that I think are 'good for them'
➡ disguise advice as a question
➡ mentor
➡ teach.

Non-directive revolves around the premise that 'the thinker' (the person you are coaching) is, as mentioned previously, 'creative, resourceful and whole' (Whitworth et al. 1998) – that they have the answers within them.

I refer to the people I work with in coaching as 'thinkers', a term coined by Nancy Kline (2002) when she wrote about the 'Thinking

Environment' that gives people time to think. In coaching, we want to encourage the thinker to do just that – to think! To build that thinking muscle so they can be independent, critical decision makers when we're not there with them, just as much as when we are.

My definition of coaching, devised in collaboration with a group of coaches on my mentor-coaching programme, is: 'A joint endeavour to move beyond known thinking to discover new thinking that energises the thinker to change.'

The principal elements of this definition are that coaching:

➡ is a joint endeavour – a partnership and adult–adult relationship (versus parent–child or master–apprentice)
➡ moves beyond known thinking – because that known thinking has kept the person where they are, and will continue to do so, if we stay in that space of known thinking with them
➡ discovers new thinking – because this leads to new ways of being and doing
➡ energises change – the very point of coaching, which makes it different from any other conversations we might have in life.

This idea of developing the independent, critical decision maker was one that I nurtured and encouraged in the leaders of Accenture. I worked there for 17 years from 1997 until 2014, mostly in leadership development roles. The best leadership isn't about telling others what to do; it's about asking others how they would approach something, so that they can build their ability to think for themselves. Telling infantilises and disempowers: it perpetuates the cycle of them asking what they should do because they lack belief in their own capacity to think. Asking them to think enables them to develop their own point of view, and grow into the best version of themselves.

This is why I use the term 'thinker'. But it's not just the head that does the thinking; the whole body is part of the thinking, as we shall discover. I've heard others call them 'the explorer' or the 'meaning-maker', which I like too.

What you can unlock through mentor-coaching and letting go of old scripts

In the course of my work as a mentor-coach for the International Coaching Federation (ICF), I've observed and given feedback on more than 700 hours of coaching conducted by more than 200 coaches. The ICF (2022) describes mentor-coaching as follows:

> Mentor Coaching for an ICF Credential consists of coaching and feedback in a collaborative, appreciative and dialogued process based on an observed or recorded coaching session to increase the coach's capability in coaching, in alignment with the ICF Core Competencies.

I define mentor-coaching as 'observed coaching with feedback against a set of competencies, which sharpens the coach's all-round presence' (Norman 2018).

The observation of our coaching is vital. It's rare, once we finish our training, that we get feedback from a third party other than the people with whom we work, who may or may not know what masterful coaching looks, sounds and feels like. Experienced mentor-coaches can watch coaches live or use recordings, and shine a light on what Eckstein (1969) calls our 'blind-, deaf- and dumb-spots',* enabling us to become aware of our limiting mindsets and put new ones in place that lead to different habits and behaviours:

➡ 'Blind spots' are those things we don't see in ourselves (a mindset or script), or don't see ourselves doing or not doing (a habit or a behaviour).
➡ 'Deaf spots' are those things we don't hear ourselves or others saying or not saying.
➡ 'Dumb spots' are the things we don't share out loud, whether that's our intuition, a challenge or direct feedback to the thinker.

---

* While the term 'blind spot' is a well-understood phrase in self-development, coaching and driving, the terms 'deaf and dumb spots' are not, so I will use the word 'blind spot' to mean gaps in self-awareness, things we are unable to discern in ourselves and our way of being, and in using this phrase 'blind spot', I mean no offence to those who are visually impaired.

A competency provides standards and measures for what to do and how to do it. Each coaching body has its own set of competencies that it expects its coaches to align with. I've included the ICF competencies (2019) in Appendix 1 for reference, so you can get a feel for what a competency is. I've also included the Professional Certified Coach (PCC) Markers (Appendix 2), which take the competencies to a more granular, measurable level. I reference the PCC Markers throughout the text. The ICF describes the Markers as 'indicators that an assessor is trained to listen for to determine which ICF Core Competencies are evident in a recorded coaching conversation and to what extent. The Markers are behaviours that represent demonstration of the Core Competencies in a coaching conversation at the PCC level. These Markers support a performance evaluation process that is fair, consistent, valid, reliable, repeatable and defensible'.

When we work with a masterful mentor-coach, all of the feedback is related to the competencies and evidence-based rather than subjective. There is nowhere to hide when we're being observed and given feedback against a set of competencies. It's such a rich learning experience. The result is greater presence in the coach, deeper thinking by the people we work with, and a more transformational experience for those people.

It's been a privilege to support and challenge coaches as they sharpen their edge. Through this process, I've noticed patterns that aren't useful to the thinkers we work with, that don't enable them to think deeply and prevent them from having the most transformational experience possible.

These patterns seemed to be habits formed because of scripts we learned in our other life roles – roles such as child, student, worker, coach in training or member of society. I started to get curious. What were people saying to us (explicitly or implicitly) at those times in our lives that led us to these beliefs and habitual patterns? People like our parents or carers, teachers, peers, managers or coach trainers?

I noticed, for example, that our parents and other carers taught us that it was rude to interrupt. That may be correct in normal conversation, but in coaching, it can be of service to interrupt the thinker's storytelling to check whether it's useful to *them* to say it out loud. I noticed that teachers often taught us to be logical and follow a set path to solving problems; yet our much-less-logical intuition can play such a powerful part in bringing new insights to the thinkers with whom we partner.

As I was preparing to draft the book, I interviewed 26 coaches across several cultures. I wanted to be sure that the mindsets and beliefs that I learned from childhood through to adulthood were representative of others' experiences, and that you'd recognise the mindsets yourself. I realise there are many cultures not represented across those 26 coaches. Nonetheless, I was surprised at how similar our experiences were, and that there were broad areas of agreement.

That said, some of the mindsets described in this book will feel consistent with what you have learned in your own life, while others may not. You may have other mindsets and beliefs that speak more to your own upbringing too. I don't claim to have come up with an exhaustive list here. In fact, I uncover more limiting mindsets each time I mentor-coach – it's a never-ending voyage of discovery. These mindsets served us at the time, and we were taught them for a reason.

But it's time to rewire the things we have learned through life and work, removing those old scripts so we can be extraordinary coaches. We need to unencumber ourselves of our old scripts, discarding and replacing them with fresh ones. I encourage every coach to come back for more mentor-coaching year-on-year, to uncover more limiting mindsets and make changes accordingly.

My purpose

I'm here to make (organisational) life more human, one thinker or team at a time. You also may be in the business of making life more human, one thinker or team at a time. In that endeavour, I'm committed to your uniqueness as a coach. You are like no other coach out there. At the same time, I'm committed to high-quality coaching, and have an eye for detail when it comes to the language you use. Language that enables the thinker to become an independent, critical decision maker.

In 2020, I wrote that mentor-coaching is for life, not just credentialling (Norman 2020). I'm planting the seed of investing in mentor-coaching – being observed as you coach, and discussing how usefully (or not) you show up for the thinker. This allows you to become conscious about the scripts that inform your habits, to shine a light on your 'blind spots' and make some small tweaks in your coaching that will make a big difference to the thinker with whom you partner – breaking away from the old scripts that may (or may not) be useful in life, but are not so useful in coaching.

I'm fascinated by the idea of marginal gains. Taking the lead from Formula 1, where every second counts, I'm constantly on the lookout for marginal gains in coaching. Not to shave off time (although in some instances, it could be to give maximum time to the thinker to think); instead, to create the best thinking environment for them so they can do their best thinking.

Everything that we do or say as coaches has an impact on that thinking environment, but it all starts with mindset. Our mindset needs to shift before our skillset can follow. By the way, the ICF recently introduced a new coaching competency called 'Embodies a coaching mindset'. The overarching definition is as follows: the coach 'develops and maintains a mindset that is open, curious, flexible and client-centred'. It goes on to say that the coach 'acknowledges that clients are responsible for their own choices' (ICF 2019). This is what we are aiming for by way of our central mindset.

How to use this book for continuous professional development

I trust that you've picked up this book because it feels relevant to you and your development right now. I hope I can help you to build on your prior learning in a way that engages and inspires you.

Each Shift covers:

➡ the old mindset of the coach
➡ how that old mindset gets in the way of facilitating the thinker to discover their own new thinking
➡ the more useful mindset that encourages new thinking
➡ the skillset – how that looks or sounds.

You may notice some repetition across the scripts: that's because we learn best by, among other things, building on prior knowledge and mental models, applying what we know in different contexts (Brown et al. 2014).

If you would like to see all the mindset Shifts in one place, flick forward to page 235. The purpose of these pages is to enable you to refind mindset Shifts that you want to revisit a second or third or fourth time. I have given you the page numbers to make that easy for you. And yes, I do recommend revisiting them, just like you might dip back into a recipe book or an encyclopaedia to find that one Shift that you particularly want to reground yourself in.

Please approach the book with a growth mindset (Dweck 2017). A fixed mindset would constitute learning to pass an exam or get to the next level of credential, ticking that off your list. A growth mindset is much more about becoming the best coach you can be.

We coaches love continuous professional development: if you put in the work to make the changes in mindset and skillset, you'll enhance the thinking environment for each one of the thinkers with whom you're partnering.

A work-related book is only as good as the changes you make as a result of reading it. I can't make you change, but I hope that you'll read with a view to changing.

To that end, I've included a retrieval practice after each section. This is one way in which we retain our learning:

> We tend to think that most learning occurs during the initial encoding stage – when students get information 'in'... However... a significant amount of learning occurs when students pull information 'out' through retrieval practice. Retrieval practice will help you to 'use it or lose it'. (Agarwal and Bain 2019)

Struggling to retrieve information is a good thing for learning – and is in fact a desirable difficulty – so don't give up just because you are finding it hard to remember what you read, give yourself time. In addition to all of that, retrieval practice will improve your understanding of your own learning process, so it has multiple benefits.

Please don't gloss over these retrieval practices. If you do, you'll be doing yourself and the thinkers a disservice because you'll forget much of what you've read, and not make the requisite changes. If you keep a continuous professional development journal for credentialling or other purposes, perhaps you might write your notes there.

I also encourage you to put the book down after each section and practise what you have learned. Bite-sized, spaced practice will help you to cement the learning (Brown et al. 2014) before moving on to the next section and committing to more bite-sized, spaced practice and building layer-upon-layer of better coaching.

James Clear, who wrote *Atomic Habits* (2018), would encourage you to give yourself some kind of trigger or cue to remind yourself in the moment to practise whatever it is you wish to try out. For example, it might be a sticky note or a photo that represents the different mindset or behaviour, or an object right in front of you as you're coaching. Whatever works for you.

Experiment. Play. Fail and learn. This is where the commitments questions will support you to name what you wish to experiment with, want to try out or stop doing. As ex-media CEO-turned-author Margaret Heffernan (2020) writes: 'The great advantage of experiments is that they stop you being stuck; they're one way to prototype the future.'

I say again: experiment, play, fail and learn. And then reward yourself! That immediate reward will entice you to repeat the experiment. I can't tell you what to reward yourself with – that's entirely up to you; but James Clear would tell you to make it immediate, so that you connect it to the new habit and then have the anticipation of reward next time, making it more likely to happen again.

Hard is good when it comes to trying out new ways of being and doing things. I encourage you not to give up, but to put in the emotional investment to make changes. Work with a mentor-coach to get feedback from outside of yourself, as you'll doubtless have 'blind spots' that you don't even know you need to do something about.

And with that, enjoy the learning. If you want further reading, all of the references are in the bibliography – but read this book first! And put the experiments into practice. Integration into your practice is key.

Chapter 1

Mindsets we learned from our parents or carers that we need to discard to be a more masterful coach

Most of us have much to be grateful for in terms of what our parents or carers taught us to keep us safe and secure. They did their best with what they had to create environments where we could flourish. Their teachings shaped us to become the adults we are today.

As you think about the messages that your parents or carers imparted, both spoken and unspoken, what did they teach you that you've needed to shake off to be a more masterful coach?

 Shift 1

OLD MINDSET: Do what I tell you to do
NEW MINDSET: Provide psychological safety so the thinker can figure out their next move

Since my parents wanted to keep me and my brother safe as children, they told us what to do and when. This was right for the time, as we learned about safety. Perhaps this resonates with you too, as it did with the coaches I interviewed.

But according to my friends who have children, there comes a time when teenagers no longer want their parents telling them what to do. There is a bit (or a lot) of rebellion, because they're testing out the limits for themselves. I can't say that I was ever particularly rebellious myself, but my brother was (that's not my story to tell, though).

I know that some adult children still like to ask their parents for advice. But we coaches aren't parents to the thinkers with whom we partner, and our role is not to give advice. No matter what our own life experiences, we can't possibly know what's best for this individual in their context, given their values and environment. They might not know either, but it's in their own gift to figure that out, with us as their sounding board – and yes, even if they have fewer life experiences than us, because it's their life, not ours or anyone else's. They might try to hook us into giving them our perspective because that's what they've always done with their parents, but our role is to create psychological safety within which they can work out their own next move.

What does that mean: psychological safety? It's a term often attributed to Amy Edmondson (1999) about how to create enough safety for teams to learn together. She cites Schein and Bennis (1965), who noticed that individuals need to feel psychologically safe to be capable of change – the purpose of coaching!

In coaching, that psychological safety might include:

➡ partnering to co-create a solid enough contract – a container, as William Isaacs (1999) calls it, within which the work can happen (see also Shifts 2 and 3)

➡ understanding the boundaries of the work – e.g. coaching, not counselling, mentoring, consulting or teaching, and the boundaries of the way we'll work (how many sessions, how often, how long, timekeeping, preparation, etc.) (see also Shifts 2, 5, 11 and 48)
➡ a nurturing environment, which doesn't stray into rescuing (Karpman 1968)
➡ inviting, noticing, accepting the whole of who they are
➡ truthful feedback, both challenging and supportive (see also Shifts 5, 6 and 55).

Winnicott termed this the 'holding environment' (Abram 2007). There's an expression in coaching that we 'hold space' for the thinker to do their best thinking, which perhaps comes from this idea of the holding environment. They need to feel that they can be vulnerable, and say anything and everything without shame or embarrassment, that would be useful to them to get to new thinking.

In the words of Brené Brown (2015), 'vulnerability is the birthplace of innovation, creativity and change', and 'shame corrodes the very part of us that believes we are capable of change'. Hence the need to create a safe space for them to be vulnerable without shame. But as mentioned previously, creating a safe space for thinkers to be vulnerable isn't about rescuing them; as Karpman (1968) puts it: we don't do the work for them to make things less effortful for them.

It's so easy to slip out of resourcing (Choy 1990) and into rescuing; but rescuing is much more parent-to-child than adult-to-adult partnering (Berne 1964): it pushes the rescued thinker into victim mode (Karpman 1968), disempowering them from thinking and acting for themselves. Instead, we need to enable them to voice (Choy 1990) their needs, ideas, insights and intentions for themselves. To be the adult of their own life.

How do you create this nurturing, resourcing environment, over and above the ideas outlined above?

➡ Give them space to work out loud – which Stepper (2020) has shown to be more effective than thinking inside the head.
➡ Give them silence when you can see they're still thinking.

The clues as to whether they're thinking lie in where they're looking, and the pace at which they're speaking. They won't be looking at you when they're thinking; they're much more likely to be looking anywhere else in the room. Their pace of speaking will have slowed, as they try to access the new thinking. It won't be on the tip of their tongue or the front of their mind if they haven't gone there before, so you need to give them enough silence to tap into that new thinking.

➡ Ask questions that move their thinking forward, rather than focusing on information-gathering questions which prompt known thinking.

➡ Challenge them.

Although I use the word 'nurturing', which might imply being supportive, resourcing is not synonymous with only being supportive. Resourcing also means being challenging (see also Shifts 5 and 29), which you can do more of if you're also supportive (Daloz 1986), giving them what Blakey and Day (2012) describe as the 'loving boot' towards high performance rather than just a cosy chat, which is nowhere near as resourcing.

None of this includes telling them what to do. It's all about enabling the thinker to change in ways that will serve them.

 # Shift 2

OLD MINDSET: Only children need boundaries
NEW MINDSET: Adults need boundaries too

Not every parent agrees these days, but when I was growing up, my parents were keen on setting boundaries. They limited where I could and couldn't go with or without them, told me not to talk to strangers, not to play too close to any edge (of water, a pavement or cliff), how much TV I could watch and which programmes, when I needed to go to bed, what was right and wrong, when enough was enough!

This was, and still is, healthy. As children, we need to have guard rails within which we feel a sense of safety. These become ground rules that we later test and push up against.

Adults need boundaries too. When we're in coaching mode, we don't need to discard this mindset at all, as long as we look at boundaries that are relevant to coaching. Contracting is the most obvious place where we discuss and agree on boundaries:

➡ What is coaching? What is it not?
➡ Where does coaching stop and therapy start – or mentoring and teaching?
➡ How often and where shall we meet, and for what duration?
➡ What are the recommendations for preparation and reflection time before and afterwards?
➡ What is the cost of the coaching?
➡ When is payment due?
➡ What happens if there's an emergency that means the thinker (or indeed the coach) is unable to come to coaching?
➡ What constitutes an emergency?
➡ What happens if they're late to the coaching session?
➡ What is our confidentiality agreement? What are the exceptions to confidentiality?
➡ What will be shared with the sponsor of the coaching, and by whom?
➡ Where might the thinker choose to locate themselves if the work is virtual, so that they're least likely to be interrupted, overheard

or overlooked and to be able to get to fresh thinking away from their usual chair (see also Shift 72)?

➡ Will we record the sessions for one or both parties to learn from?

➡ How we'll work together – for example, how much support and challenge would be useful, how much experimentation are they willing to try, whether we can interrupt them in service of new thinking?

➡ Who will their accountability buddy be to keep them on-track – setting them up for independence when we're no longer collaborating with them?

Those are what I call the 'Big C Contract'. You both need to be clear on these boundaries so they feel safe to do the work with you and both feel protected should something untoward happen. Then there's the 'little c contract' – the contract for each session (see also Shift 3). This is more about partnering to figure out:

➡ what this session is about, what we'll cover and leave out

➡ how we'll know we have been successful by the time we finish the session

➡ how we'll work together to generate new thinking in this session – revisiting the amount of challenge and support they would like about this particular issue, and revisiting permission to interrupt

➡ how long we have together.

I know that some people are loathe to set a time limit for their coaching sessions, seeing this as restrictive and reductionist. But having the boundary of time counter-intuitively leads to more ideas, insights and intentions rather than fewer. I've lost count of the number of times that a thinker has had a revelation just after I've said: 'We have 10 minutes left to us; what would be most useful to you now?' That mention of time appears to kick the brain up a notch. The boundary of time is critical to new thinking (see also Shift 11).

Boundaries create psychological safety and a container without which the thinking cannot be done.

📊 Shift 3

OLD MINDSET: You should always try your hardest

NEW MINDSET: This should be hard work for the thinker, not for the coach

For many of us, our parents taught us about the importance of trying hard (and if we didn't learn this from them, perhaps we learned it from school). Some also encouraged perfection and top marks. While that was important at school and then at work, trying hard as a coach can get in the way of our partnership with the thinker.

The key word here is partnership. Coaching is a *joint endeavour* to move beyond known thinking to discover new thinking that energises the thinker to change.

Within that joint endeavour, the coach has responsibility for holding the process that enables new thinking to happen. The thinker for whom we're holding that process has responsibility for thinking for themselves and moving forward. Too often, I notice the coach taking too much responsibility on their shoulders for pushing the thinker forwards: they're trying too hard.

Perhaps they're:

➡ looking for the 'perfect' question (hint: there is no such thing)
➡ feeling pressure to drive to a solution by the end of the session (see also Shifts 15 and 45)
➡ leading where the session goes
➡ taking the burden of thinking that should be firmly the thinker's (the clue is in the title – 'thinker').

The harder the coach works, the less hard the thinker will think.

The mindset needed is vastly different to trying hard yourself: encouraging the thinker to work hard instead. Nobody ever promised that being coached was easy – it isn't. Claire Pedrick (2020) says 'there is discomfort in discovery', and that's absolutely right: it can be scary to find out new things about ourselves and to change

7

who we are, what we believe and what we want from life.

Coaching requires effort on the part of the thinker. It requires their full participation. It requires them to take responsibility for the demanding work of thinking, delving underneath the surface, going beyond the obvious. Like Thomas Edison (1932) once said about 'genius', it's 99 per cent perspiration, 1 per cent inspiration – so as a coach, help them to help themselves by making them do the work!

There may be something else wrapped up in this. Maybe you have the idea that the coach should be a service provider rather than a partner (see also Shift 38 to understand the connection). But in essence, the coach needs the mindset of partner, not service provider.

What does this look and sound like, encouraging them to do the work? First, asking 'contracting' questions that get them to think hard about exactly what they want from this coaching session, and not letting them off the hook with something woolly or a request that you decide for them, based on what others have brought to coaching in the past.

I use the acronym CONTRACT to integrate these contracting questions, which are mapped to the ICF competencies '3: Establishes and Maintains Agreements' and '5: Maintains Presence':

Check-in: 'What would be most useful to think about today?'
Objective: 'What would you like to be different by the time we finish today?'
Necessity: 'What is it about this that's important to you right now?'
Time: 'What is your specific question for today's X minutes?'
Realisation: 'How will you know you've got what you need by the time we wrap up today?'
Agenda: 'What is your sense of what we need to cover today to get to your outcome?'
Co-creation: 'How would you like us to work together today?' 'How much challenge are you up for?' 'May I have permission to interrupt in service of new thinking?'
Their agenda: 'Where shall we start?'

As you can see, right from the start, these questions aren't always easy for the thinker to answer. But they are necessary. We spend time getting the question for the session clear before moving on, just like Albert Einstein or an unnamed Yale academic purportedly said, 'If I had an hour to solve a problem... I would spend the first 55 minutes determining the proper question to ask... for once I know the proper question, I could solve the problem in less than five minutes' (Quote Investigator 2014).

Let's dissect each of the elements of CONTRACT for a moment to understand why they're important.

Check-in: 'What would be most useful to think about today?'
'The coach partners with the client to identify or reconfirm what the client wants to accomplish in this session' (PCC Marker 3.1; ICF 2020).

➡ This is the thinker's thinking time, so they need to decide what they wish to think about.
➡ 'Useful' – also could be replaced by 'important' or 'meaningful' – is leaning into thinking about concerns or opportunities that are significant for the thinker.
➡ 'Think about' – we signal that this is a thinking time and space, a place to go deeper.

Objective: 'What would you like to be different by the time we finish today?'
'The coach partners with the client to identify or reconfirm what the client wants to accomplish in this session' (PCC Marker 3.1; ICF 2020).

➡ This takes the answer to the first question deeper.
➡ 'Different' – signifies that something will change or shift within the session. This is not about going around in circles, as we often do in non-coaching conversations.
➡ 'Today' – focuses on where the thinker wishes to be by the end of the session, not by the time they've taken action outside of the session, although this could be a great additional question: 'If you could resolve this, what would be different for you in your life/work/relationship?'
➡ You may wish to turbo-charge this question by asking: 'If this coaching were to be transformational for you today, what would be a great outcome?'

Necessity: 'What is it about this that's important to you right now?'
'Coach enquires or explores what is important or meaningful to the client about what they want to accomplish in this session' (PCC Marker 3.3; ICF 2020).

➡ This question peels the onion even further and gets to more new thinking for the thinker.

➡ It aims to check that this really is important to the thinker, and may lead them to something that is more important to them.

➡ In my experience, this question can often be a trigger for any emotion that's attached to their concern or opportunity. This is when we know that this is truly important for them: it enables us to work at an emotional, 'being' level, which is more transformational than working at a 'doing' level.

➡ I've also started to ask: 'What is it about this that's important to who you are?', as this supports the thinker to articulate their values and get beyond the transactional.

➡ Notice that this doesn't start with 'Why...' because this can suggest judgement and invite defensiveness to justify their reason.

Time: 'What is your specific question for today's X minutes?'
'The coach partners with the client to identify or reconfirm what the client wants to accomplish in this session' (PCC Marker 3.1; ICF 2020).

➡ Framing what they want as a one-sentence question gives focus for the session.

➡ If the thinker has been wordy up until now, you could precede this question with: '*In one sentence*, what is your specific question for today's X minutes?'

➡ Naming the time frame supports the thinker to choose the element of the bigger piece of work that's most important to think about today. We can adapt this question by asking: 'If one element were most important for us to focus on in our X minutes, what would it be?'

➡ Yes, this might feel repetitive, but together you're getting clearer on what you're there to work on. (In my experience, the thinker doesn't receive the question as a repeat, but as a crystallisation of what they wish to think about.)

➡ Note that we mention time *after* the thinker has articulated what is most important to them to work on, so they don't limit what they bring to coaching. Think of this like a funnel, where they start big and get increasingly channelled. Starting at the top of the funnel means that they see the whole picture before deciding which element is most important. If you state the time you have together at the very start of the session, you risk limiting them to something less impactful, as they might choose something that they perceive to be easier, less risky or smaller, rather than the most important concern or opportunity.

Realisation: 'How will you know you've got what you need by the time we wrap up today?'

'Coach partners with the client to define or reconfirm measure(s) of success for what the client wants to accomplish in this session' (PCC Marker 3.2; ICF 2020).

➡ This question gives us even more focus on exactly what success looks, feels and sounds like. Every robust outcome has a measure of success, so that we recognise it when we see it or feel it or sense it.

➡ You might wish to ask additional questions that get at the feeling, as many thinkers go straight to a list, steps or ideas when the feelings associated with those are just as important. 'How will you feel as a result of having [that measure]?' or 'What will you feel in your body that tells you that [that measure] will be useful?"

➡ 'What will that give you?' or 'How will that be useful to you?' might be useful follow-up questions.

➡ If they say they want a plan, don't assume that you know what a plan is for them. Follow up with another question, such as: 'What does a plan look like for you?' The same may be said for other measures of success: check in as to exactly what that is for the thinker with whom you're working.

➡ This layer gives both coach and thinker a measure that you can check back on at the end of the session. For example: 'You said that you wanted X; where are you now?'

Agenda: 'What is your sense of what we need to cover today to get to your outcome?'

'Coach partners with the client to define what the client believes they need to address to achieve what they want to accomplish in this session' (PCC Marker 3.4; ICF 2020).

➡ This is like an agenda question, giving the thinker an outline of where they might take the session.

➡ An alternative question might be 'What's in scope today and what is out of scope?'

➡ This is useful when you recontract part-way through a session and say: 'What are you aware of now that you weren't aware of at the start of our session?' Give them space to answer, then: 'Where would be most useful to explore now?' The original agenda answers may guide them as to where to go next – or they may have discovered a different route to get to what's most important to them.

Co-creation: 'How would you like us to work together today?'
'Coach partners with the client by supporting the client to choose what happens in this session' (PCC Marker 5.3; ICF 2020).

➡ This is about the partnership. Note that you're asking: 'How would you like *us* to work together?', not: 'How would you like *me* to work with you?'

➡ If the thinker answers in terms of what they want from you as their coach, you might wish to follow this question up with: 'And how do *you* wish to be today to get the most from the time we have together?' You might also wish to ask: 'What might get in the way of your best thinking today, that we may need to attend to right now?'

➡ You could also follow up with: 'How much challenge are you up for?' so you can gauge how tender or robust they are, and so how receptive they are to challenge. If they say: 'Lots of challenge,' follow up with something along the lines of: 'How will we know that we're challenging enough for you?' or 'Please say at any point if you want more challenge or less,' as this demonstrates: 'Coach partners with the client by inviting the client to respond in any way to the coach's contributions and accepts the client's response' (PCC Marker 4.4; ICF 2020).

➡ 'May I have permission to interrupt in service of new thinking?' The answer to this question can help you as coach to feel freer to interrupt (see also Shift 4). It alerts the thinker to expect interruption, rather than being perturbed by it. It also alerts them to the fact that, as mentioned previously, coaching is about new thinking, not known thinking.

Their Agenda: 'Where shall we start?'
'Coach partners with the client by supporting the client to choose what happens in this session' (PCC Marker 5.3; ICF 2020).

➡ You're handing the reins to the thinker to go wherever their thinking is already taking them.
➡ If you ask a question at this time, it's likely to be one that takes them in a different direction from where their head is already taking them. Inadvertently, you'll be taking them away from their train of thought. Their train of thought is paramount.
➡ If they're hesitant in reaction to this question, you may wish to ask: 'Where else might we start? And where else?' so they have some options to choose from. Don't presume that you should jump in with a question to rescue them from not knowing: ask them to think for themselves.

I hope this answers any questions or objections you might have about those CONTRACTing questions. You're building the thinking muscles in the thinker, enabling them to think harder than they may ever have thought before. Thinking is a necessity in coaching, not a nicety. Continue to enable the thinker to think and try hard, rather than trying hard yourself.

When you don't know where you are in the middle of the conversation (a good thing, by the way – the best coaches are OK with not knowing), recontract rather than take responsibility for deciding the direction that you both take. Recontracting might sound like:

➡ 'What do you sense now that you didn't sense at the beginning?'
➡ 'What's explicit now that wasn't explicit before?'
➡ 'What's evident now that wasn't evident when we started?'

Then follow up with:

➡ 'With that in mind, where do we need to explore next?'
➡ Or find your own alternatives that are authentic for you.

This recontracting keeps the responsibility for the direction of the conversation firmly with the thinker. This is *their* coaching and *their* life, so you need to give them the choice about which direction would be most useful to them. If you're unsure, you might ask: 'Is this useful to you?' If not: 'What do we need to think about next?' or 'What *would* be more useful to think about?'

Don't guess whether a direction is useful to them – ask.

These kinds of questions will keep you out of both the content and driving to a solution. You might think this is the role of the coach – to get to a solution to the problem or opportunity that the thinker has brought. But oftentimes, driving too hard and fast can lead to transactional actions that simply don't address the person's underlying needs. We'll come back to that in Shifts 15 and 45. We'll also come back to why you don't ask them about their progress since last time as your first question unless it's been contracted for (see also Shift 70) and how you conduct the 'Big C Contract' (see also Shift 2) and three-way contracting (see also Shift 75).

 # Shift 4

OLD MINDSET: It's rude to interrupt

NEW MINDSET: It's useful to interrupt if it enables the thinker to move away from known thinking towards new thinking

I have a vivid memory of being told off by my dad for interrupting an adult conversation when I was young: it was mortifying in front of these other adults. Of all the times that my parents urged me not to interrupt, this is the one that is the loudest in my head.

I heard similar stories from the coaches I interviewed. Does this sound familiar to you, your parents teaching you that it's rude to interrupt others when they're speaking? This had merit, as we needed to learn that not everything centred around us and our universe. When others are in conversation, we should learn to listen and bide our time before adding our thoughts. Children are often not actually part of the conversation, and their interruptions tend to be about something completely different.

This is an important lesson to learn: don't interrupt other people's flow with something completely different.

When we become coaches, we learn to listen and pay attention to what the thinker says. This is a good habit to learn – in the main. This is perhaps the first time in their lives that a thinker has been so exquisitely listened to. This helps them to feel valued and valuable. They know they have someone on their side who fully supports them. The trouble is, sometimes we can over-listen. If a thinker is telling us things they already know – the story, chronology, context, the way they've already explained it to their friend or family – then they're gaining nothing new from this time with us. They know it already.

Our job as coach is to *get them to new thinking, not to go over old ground*.

We don't need them to fill us in on all the context if they already know it themselves. They (and we) may think we need to know the detail to be able to support them, but we don't. We're not in the business of diagnosing and supplying solutions (see also Shift 63). These are the times when it *is* important to be able to interrupt: when we think that the thinker might be in the midst of telling the story.

To make this possible, adopt a different mindset. Instead of it being rude to interrupt, you need to believe that this could be useful to enable a thinker to get to new thinking. If you can enable them to cut to the chase, to 'bottom line' (Whitworth et al. 1998), you could give them more time to get to new thinking.

But how do we do that? I know of one coach who asks: 'Why are you paying me huge sums of money to talk about something you could talk to your friends about for nothing?' That might feel highly challenging for you, so here are some alternatives. First, ask during the session contracting phase: 'May I have your permission to interrupt you in service of new thinking?'

I sometimes also say, especially if I know the thinker is a storyteller: 'Please don't feel you need to fill me in on all the detail. Our job in coaching is to get you to new thinking, rather than going over old ground.' This early contracting also serves to stop them telling us about the history in the first place, so preventing the need for interruption. Once you have permission, you know that it won't be such a jolt to them if and when you do interrupt. It also gives you more courage in the moment to make that interruption because you have gained the thinker's express permission.

At the point when you suspect that the thinker might be going over old ground, or when they appear to be going round in circles, saying the same thing multiple times, interrupt. You might be thinking that they seem to be almost at the end of their story, so interrupting would take longer than letting the story take its course. However, in my experience, the story always goes on for longer than you think it will. There are peaks and troughs, highs and lows, and it's more likely they have reached the end of one of those cycles rather than the end of the whole story.

I suggest you look out for signs that the thinker is in the story. They are likely to be:

➡ talking quite fast, because they've told the story before and don't need to think about what they're saying
➡ looking at you rather than up, down or to the sides (which as

mentioned previously, usually indicates they're thinking new thoughts).

You might not feel there's a long enough pause to interrupt, so you may need to assert yourself more than you might like – remembering all the time that this is in service of their new thinking, and they have given you permission: 'May I interrupt you?' or: 'If I might interrupt you for a moment...'

Then follow that up with something like:

➡ 'It sounds as though you might know this already?' Pause for them to reflect. 'If so, please don't feel you need to fill me in on the detail. Is this useful to you to say this out loud?' If they say yes, great, that's now their conscious choice.

➡ 'If you know this already, how do we get you from known thinking to new thinking?'

➡ 'Is this giving you new insights?' Pause to allow them to answer. If no: 'Where do we need to go to get new insights?' If yes, keep going.

➡ 'What is the essence of this story?'

➡ 'What is the learning for you from this story?'

➡ 'What is the bottom line here?'

Or find words that feel natural to you. Know that interrupting will feel uncomfortable to begin with, and don't stop doing it just because you hear your parents' or other carer's voice saying: 'It's rude to interrupt.' It will become easier over time, particularly when you start to see how much further the thinker can get in a session if you use the time for new rather than known thinking.

If you're still worried that you might miss something by short-cutting to the essence of the story versus the detail, bear in mind that you have a whole session ahead of you to pay attention to their body language, tone, terminology, metaphors, emotions, beliefs and assumptions.

☺ Shift 5

OLD MINDSET: Don't talk back

NEW MINDSET: Challenge assumptions, offer disruptive reflections and insight into 'blind spots'

Many cultures instruct children to respect much wiser elders. That includes not talking back, not disagreeing or arguing with them. Besides which, as the old saying goes: 'Children should be seen and not heard.' This is sometimes carried forward into our adult lives, where we hold on to feedback that could be useful to the other person. I don't just mean to our elders, either; I notice leaders keeping silent for fear of upsetting their people, peers not offering feedback to peers, and coaches not offering feedback to the thinkers with whom they're partnering.

In all of these roles, it's our duty to offer feedback: that's not talking back at all; it's being useful. I realise that this can be tricky, as you don't want to be hurtful. That's another mindset to discard – that offering feedback is hurtful or leads to conflict (see also Shift 6).

If we offer feedback from a place of positive intent and with love, we're being useful. Will this challenge, disruptive reflection or insight be useful to the growth of the thinker? If the answer to this is yes, you're doing them a disservice by withholding it. This needs to come from a place of partnership, not power. We're not standing in judgement of them; rather, offering something that could be helpful to them, related to what they're bringing to coaching.

We can use the model of 'I'm OK, you're OK', developed by Harris (1967), subsequently built on by Ernst (1971) to stand in this space of equals. 'I'm OK, you're OK' is a balanced, healthy belief to hold, which assumes 'I am OK and you are OK as well'. For example, if the thinker comes from a place of 'I'm not OK, you're OK', you'll notice they give you too much power in the way they speak to you, minimising or discounting themselves and maximising you, deferring to your perceived greater wisdom. If this is to be a partnership, it would be useful to hold up a mirror to them and ask them how they can reclaim their 'OK-ness' in this relationship.

Speaking of partnership, you will have contracted for levels of challenge within your 'Big C Contract' before the coaching programme starts, then again at the start of each coaching session. The level of challenge that the thinker has capacity for may change from session to session. If they come to coaching one day feeling particularly tender, it's important they feel they can ask you to be more supportive than challenging on that day; equally, if they're feeling really robust that day, they need the opportunity to tell you that they'd like higher levels of challenge.

Always contract for how they'd like to work together (see the Co-creation element of CONTRACT and Shift 3).

There is a scale of magnitude in challenge. At the safer end of the spectrum, for example, might be something like: 'This feels quite pacy; how is it for you?' (If indeed that's how it's feeling). This could be useful for them to ponder. What is causing the pace, what can they learn from it? How do they want to harness or slow it?

> Or: 'I notice your face twitched when you said that. What is the insight for you?'
> Or: 'I hear you say you plan to do that, but your tone of voice suggests otherwise. What are your thoughts?'
> Or: 'I get a sense that there's something you're not saying to yourself? If so, what might that be?'

You'll notice that those examples covered feeling, seeing, hearing and sensing. Also, that each observation is followed by an enquiry to explore their thinking on the matter, so the thinker can make meaning of it (or not, if you haven't quite captured it).

You might feel challenged yourself when the thinker shows up to the session without having prepared, turning up late as a pattern of behaviour and not taking the actions they said they'd take. It can be tricky to get the balance right here, to challenge them to make the most of the process. At the end of the day it's their responsibility to take action and prepare – or not. It's frustrating for us as we see the missed opportunities. However, you're not their teacher, standing in judgement over whether they've done their homework. These are things we can contract for, though, as part of our 'Big C Contract' conversation: we can refer back to that contract if it would be useful to them.

For example:

'I'm noticing a pattern of late arrival to our meetings. I'm wondering whether that's representative of how you show up for other meetings, and how that feels for you?'

Or:

'I'm noticing that you've come to the last two sessions without something specific to think about. I'm wondering whether that's a pattern for you in your work, and how that's working for you?'

If they wish to do something about the pattern, you can work with that. If they don't, and it doesn't contravene your boundaries for working, let it go.

Our parents or carers might also have taught us that wearing our hearts on our sleeves could be detrimental to us, as others might take advantage as a result. Telling others how we felt because of their actions might make us come across as weak. As we moved into adulthood, we might have held on to these beliefs, informing our actions – or rather, our silence.

For coaches, this is rich material from which to offer feedback to the thinker. If you're experiencing the person in front of you in a certain way, the chances are that others have experienced them similarly. It's quite possible that no one has ever given them this feedback, yet it could be incredibly useful to them. Not saying what you're experiencing (seeing, feeling, hearing, sensing) is a missed opportunity for learning and growth for the thinker.

Here's one example:

'One of your goals for coaching is to become more succinct in the way you present, and I notice that I find it hard to follow your train of thought. I wonder whether that's how it feels for your usual audience. What do you think?'

More challenging for you – and for the thinker – might be something like:

'I'm finding that I'm bored as you talk about this, and I'm wondering how *you* feel about this subject?'

Each of these examples comes up in the moment. They're not prescribed in advance, but come from our sensing and intuition. If you notice it, don't leave it unsaid, as it could be really useful to them, even if somewhat challenging.

Your role is to be challenging, to disrupt and shine a light on 'blind-spots', not to have a cosy chat (see also Shifts 5 and 25).

♟ Shift 6

OLD MINDSET: If you can't say something nice, don't say anything at all

NEW MINDSET: Offer a ratio of 5.6:1 positive-to-constructive feedback

Here's an expression you may have heard a lot when you were growing up: 'If you can't say something nice (to your brother, sister, friend or classmate), don't say anything at all.'

I understand this sentiment from other children saying hurtful things to me when I was a child. That led to another of my mum's phrases: 'Sticks and stones will break my bones, but names will never hurt me.'

As adults and coaches, we need to give constructive feedback sometimes in service of the thinker's growth. That's not about saying something nice or nasty, it's about being useful to them. If we were never to give them any feedback about how we're experiencing them, they would be missing out on useful data that others may never have shared with them. How we experience them during coaching is usually a parallel to the way others have experienced them, but those others (peers, leaders, team members) have kept it to themselves for fear of causing emotional injury – their parents' voices in their heads about saying only nice things, and not knowing how to give feedback in an objective, evidence-based way (see also Shift 55).

Kim Cameron (2012) found that in high-performing organisations, the ratio of positive-to-constructive feedback is 5.6:1. In poor-performing, struggling organisations, the ratio was as low as 0.36:1. This tells us something about the utility of offering positive feedback to thinkers, and constructive, developmental feedback (see also Shift 5). It's as important that people know what behaviour to repeat, as it is for them to understand what they might consider stopping and starting. How much positive feedback do you offer to thinkers? (See also Shift 7 about acknowledgement of who the thinker is being.)

I'm not actually advocating for 5.6 times as much positive acknowledgement compared with constructive feedback, as the coach would be inserting themselves too much into the thinking time; but I am advocating more acknowledgement and celebration than you might currently be offering. Or, as I have started to do lately, ask the thinker what they would like to celebrate in themselves, so that they own that and make it personal.

That said, it's not our role as coaches to give feedback that a line manager is responsible for giving on a day-to-day basis. We're not a conduit for something a manager finds difficult, or doesn't take the time to do – we're not an outsourced function. The feedback we give will be based on what we experience in the room with a thinker. Nothing more, nothing less, and not influenced by what others say.

(Be) Shift 7

OLD MINDSET: Mind your 'Ps and Qs'
NEW MINDSET: Acknowledge who the thinker is being in the moment

Did you know that the expression 'mind your Ps and Qs' was used by pub landlords when people were getting too rowdy? The Ps stood for pints, and the Qs stood for quarts. It has morphed into meaning 'be polite with your please and thank-yous'. Absolutely right: I can't stand impoliteness! As we build relationships and contract for coaching, courtesy is essential to grease the wheels of rapport. One way that I do this is to thank people in my invoicing emails, for their business and for investing in themselves.

However, I notice that when a coach says 'thank you' to the thinker for an answer to their question in a session, it doesn't sound right in this context. It gets in the way of the sense of equals coming together in partnership. 'Thank you for that' gets in the way of the flow for the thinker, and makes it more about the coach: it's as though we're thanking them for filling us in when, as we've already identified, the purpose of coaching is to get them to new thinking.

The same goes for saying 'sorry' if the coach makes a mistake of some kind (see Shift 8). Maybe we ask a question that doesn't land, stumble as we paraphrase or ask a stacked question (two or more questions asked in the same breath), and apologise when we realise it. Suddenly, the conversation is about us when it should be all about the thinker.

The only time I thank a thinker in a session is for bringing their whole selves 'into the room'. It's more of an acknowledgement of who they're being. The ICF competency, Cultivating Trust and Safety, suggests that the 'coach acknowledges and respects the client's unique talents, insights, and work in the coaching process' (ICF 4.3), and the 'coach acknowledges and supports the client's expression of feelings, perceptions, beliefs and suggestions' (ICF 4.5).

Acknowledgement is different from thanks. Thanks is about

politeness and encouragement to do something again for our benefit; whereas acknowledgement adds value to the thinker by calling out what they're good at, or who they're being.

This should never be about us – it's always about the thinker. For example:

➡ 'May I acknowledge your unique blend of organisational skills, empathy and vision, which differentiate you?'
➡ 'I acknowledge how deep you have gone in this session to identify your beliefs and feelings about this.'
➡ 'You sound ready to go!'

– or whatever works authentically for you, given who the thinker is being.

The next time you feel inclined to thank them for their answers, bite your tongue. Listen instead to how they're showing up, and acknowledge them for that at some point (see also Shift 25).

⊚ Shift 8

OLD MINDSET: Say 'sorry'
NEW MINDSET: Let it be OK to make mistakes in a session

I imagine your elders taught you to say 'sorry' when you made a mistake. That's certainly my experience and that of those I interviewed. As mentioned previously, I'm a big advocate of 'please', 'thank you' and 'sorry' – but not in coaching.

Why? Two reasons:

➡ It puts the attention onto you and your mistake, which stops the thinker in their thinking tracks. According to Mark et al. (2008), when thinking is interrupted, it can take up to 23 minutes to get back in flow again. That isn't good use of the thinker's thinking time if they're distracted in this way.

➡ It may make you less likely to want to make mistakes in your coaching, which in turn means you may be less likely to challenge or blurt out a half-formed question, or say what your intuition is telling you to say.

The mindset to replace this is to be OK with your own missteps, let them pass without comment and be unattached to them. Let them go.

Here are three examples where you might previously have apologised for getting it wrong: the better mindset is to be comfortable with these micro-mistakes, and let them disappear into the ether without apology. This can have the added side-effect of creating psychological safety, as you show your imperfection without making a big deal of it.

➡ Coaching is about support *and* challenge, so you can't feel afraid of challenging *too* hard. Indeed, Blakey and Day (2012) asked the thinkers with whom they worked what would give them more impact in their coaching: the majority said they would have benefited from more challenge, not less, from their coach. There's no need to be sorry for poking and prodding, especially if they've asked for this.

➡ Half-formed questions are often the most powerful, as the thinker interprets them as they see fit. Again, no need to be apologetic for not quite getting those perfect. 'Perfection is the enemy of progress,' as Winston Churchill famously said in his 1952 speech to the Conservative Party Conference.

➡ Sometimes you might worry that you can't tell the difference between your intuition and your own stuff. However, the coach who hesitates is lost – or at least, the time to utter that intuition aloud will have passed. The more you practise laying out your intuition, the more you will be able to differentiate; but even if you're not sure, as long as you say it without attachment and let it go without apology if it doesn't hit the mark, the more confident you will become.

Can you think of other times when you've apologised, and your apology ended up putting the spotlight on you and taking it off the thinker?

🖼 Shift 9

OLD MINDSET: Eye contact is polite
NEW MINDSET: Being side-by-side or audio-only allows for more vulnerability

In my culture, eye contact is considered to be polite. Not looking people in the eye is considered 'shifty' in some way. We're encouraged by our parents to look into a person's eyes to show our interest in what they're saying. I know this isn't the case in all cultures, such as Malawi, for example, where it's more polite to look away. But if you've been taught to give eye contact, this Shift will resonate.

Perhaps you notice when you're in the car with a teenager, sitting side-by-side, or washing up and drying up side-by-side, that they're more likely to open up into a more meaningful conversation than if you're sitting opposite each other at the dinner table. Side-by-side conversations work for teenagers, and they work for adults too. Side-by-side can be less intrusive than face-to-face. It allows them to be more vulnerable. There are two aspects to this:

➡ They don't feel the need to be polite and give you eye contact, according to Markson and Paterson (2009), which means they can look wherever they want to look in order to do their best thinking – up, down, sideways, wherever they can access new thinking.

➡ They don't feel intimidated by you giving them eye contact, and are more likely to relax and open up.

Camera-on web calls have meant that we have many more face-to-face conversations these days. Better to switch off the camera and opt for audio-only – or revert to good, old-fashioned phone calls instead, which are hands-free and allow for walking at the same time. If you're co-located, you can of course walk side-by-side for the same effect.

Don't get caught up in thinking you need eye contact – counter-intuitively, it can get in the way of great thinking.

✌ Shift 10

OLD MINDSET: Don't be nosy
NEW MINDSET: Do be curious on the thinker's behalf

Many of us will have been taught right from childhood not to be nosy. It just isn't the done thing to ask about someone's personal life, financial situation or religious beliefs – the list could go on. The problem is that refraining from what we might perceive to be nosy questions can stop us from supporting the thinker to get underneath the surface of their own beliefs, values and identity.

Get curious. This is curiosity not for your sake (which *would* be nosy), not to fill you in on unnecessary detail, but to fill the thinker in on the meaning. There will be things they haven't thought about in years that could have a bearing on what they're tussling with now. There will be beliefs that have shaped the way they live, which may or may not be serving them anymore in relation to this issue or opportunity. There will be values that they didn't even know they lived by – until you, the coach, ask questions that prompt *their* curiosity about these things.

You might ask questions such as:

➡ 'What is the belief that leads you to be that way?'
➡ 'What assumptions might you be making about that?'
➡ 'What is important to you about that?'
➡ 'Who do you want to be in relation to this?'
➡ 'How do you *want* to show up?'
➡ 'What are you noticing?'
➡ 'What is that about?'

You can see how these questions are not about getting context, detail or data. You don't need any of that because your role is not to solve the issue for the thinker (see also Shifts 24, 31, 39 and 52). Your role is to enable the thinker to make meaning and decipher how they want to use that meaning-making to change.

⏱ Shift 11

OLD MINDSET: It's rude to look at the clock
NEW MINDSET: We signal time checks to trigger new thinking

How did looking at the clock become rude? Something we learned that we shouldn't do for fear of offending the other person? How did it become synonymous with 'I'm ready for this conversation to be over?' I'm not sure that I ever heard my parents say out loud that it's rude to look at the time when you're with others, but it does seem to be one of those unspoken rules.

Time is precious, certainly, and we can use it wisely or not. We can make the most of time or fritter it away. I wonder whether the notion of rudeness comes from a belief that time is a scarce resource? We have the same amount of time each day and can't elongate it; but looking at the clock doesn't automatically mean we're looking to get out of a conversation sooner rather than later. The only data we can draw from it is that someone wants to know what time it is! Any further assumptions are climbing Argyris' (1990) ladder of inference, drawing conclusions that aren't necessarily true.

What *is* true in most coaching situations is that both parties have other commitments to attend to at some point after the coaching: we do need to keep track of time, so each person can pay attention to those other engagements or tasks. It's one of the boundaries that keeps us both feeling a sense of psychological safety (see also Shift 1), knowing we won't be late for the next part of our day.

However, time plays a bigger role in coaching than marking the minutes. It helps a person to think too, when they know this work is being done within a contained time. Their brain knows they have X minutes and works towards that amount of time.

As the coach you keep an eye on the time, *and* you need to enable the thinker to do the same. It's no good getting most of the way through a session, then springing it on the thinker that you have five minutes left. They will have been lost in their own thinking space and not necessarily paying attention to the time: it might come as a complete shock that they 'only' have five minutes left. I know of one thinker who held back on bringing up anything particularly emotional towards the back end of the session because she didn't know how much time she still had to process it and didn't want to open a can of worms that couldn't be recanned within the session. Not mentioning time was detrimental to her thinking process.

Keep an eye on the time, and ensure that the thinker knows where you are timewise. For example:

➡ 'What is our question for the hour we have together today?'
➡ 'We are halfway through our time together. What do you sense now that you didn't sense before?'
➡ 'You said at the beginning you wanted X. What would be most useful to you in our last X- minutes to move towards that?'
➡ 'How would you like to pull all of the threads together in our last X minutes?'

Here, notice that there's no talk of 'only' or 'just' 30 minutes or five minutes. You can do a lot together in five minutes if you have what Stephen Covey (1999) calls an 'abundance mentality' about time, rather than a 'scarcity mentality' (see also Shift 81).

As mentioned previously, what I notice is that tying time back to the contract enables the thinker to discover new thinking. A new insight or realisation often crops up in that last five minutes that didn't seem anywhere close to the surface before we talked about this being the last five minutes – so it is worth signalling time checks to trigger new thinking.

🦾 Shift 12

OLD MINDSET: Don't get too big for your boots

NEW MINDSET: Own your coaching strengths

It aggrieves me that parents use this expression: 'Don't get too big for your boots.' It can make a child retreat into themselves, make themselves small and minimise their achievements or strengths. I can't find any useful rationale for it, except in the similar expression that 'nobody likes a smart alec!'

I see coaches letting this get in their way all the time, particularly when they start coaching. They forget that they have all sorts of history that leads to them being the person – and the coach – that they are today. They're not starting from a clean slate, but from a background experience that comes in all shapes and sizes. This is what makes them unique.

I encourage all coaches to reflect on their journey-line, from birth to today:

➡ What are the pivotal moments that shaped you – the highlights and the lowlights?
➡ Who are you as a coach today because of all of the learning you have to date? Not just about coaching, but everything you have learned along the way?
➡ What is your personal matrix of strengths?

This 'don't be too much' mindset can also be confused with the mindset that we shouldn't bring our own stuff to the coaching room. That one is true: this isn't about us sharing our experiences, although we might divulge a little about our lives at the start of a session by way of building rapport. This mindset is as much about you as it is about you in partnership with a thinker.

Here's the thing: who you are is how you coach. Please own who you are. It's usually one of the questions that a potential thinker asks us in a chemistry session:

➡ 'What makes you unique as a coach?'

➡ 'What is your style of coaching?'

The journey-line is a useful exercise to go through, to enable you to articulate what makes you different from all of the other coaches out there. There are more than 100,000 LinkedIn profiles in the UK alone that have 'coach' in their title, so you need to be able to differentiate yourself and own your personal strengths.

In a recent conversation with Steve Ridgley, coach and coach supervisor, we both realised how much our hobbies influence the way we show up in coaching for example.

In the words of the 1980s anthem made famous by Gloria Gaynor: 'I am what I am.'

# Shift 13

My parents instilled in me that I shouldn't be selfish, that I should think of others before myself. My interviewees said the same about their parents' endorsement not to be selfish. As we become adults, we might unwittingly put ourselves and our own needs at the bottom of the priority list while everyone else's take precedence.

For those of us who become coaches, we need to put our own oxygen mask on first – as the aeroplane announcement advocates – before we help others. If we fail to do this, we may not be able to help others anyway, as we will have run out of oxygen. I've heard one coach say that her clients don't pay for her time; they pay for her self-care. The more she takes care of herself and her own needs outside of coaching, the better resourced she is to resource the thinkers with whom she works.

This is the mindset we need to adopt. It's not selfish; it's about being self-centred in order to be thinker-centred when we're with them.

➡ What would it take to resource yourself, so you have the capacity to work at your best for every thinker?
➡ How do you want to structure your days, so you get enough recuperation time in between coaching?

I know of one senior leader who felt that internal coaches could (and should) coach back-to-back for eight hours a day. I can't see how the second thinker benefited from that approach, let alone the eighth or the one at the end of the week. I notice that some coaches do schedule high numbers of sessions per day to feel productive: that's perhaps a residue from their days within an organisation, where time needed to be used productively – meaning fitting as much in as humanly possible, earning as much as possible.

We need to be careful not to be driven by earning more money if that means that thinkers get a lesser presence from us. What would it be like for the eighth person in a day – or even the sixth? And what about our own health?

The problem with fitting in as many people as we can per day is that coaching takes a different kind of energy. As we've already seen, it's not that we work especially hard as the coach – that's the job of the thinker (see Shifts 3 and 27). But being present for the thinker takes a different kind of energy. I doubt that we are that present in many other kinds of meetings or conversations. Keeping focused on the thinker means that you can't work with eight people, one after the other. You need some downtime in between, which enables you to clear your mind of the earlier thinker so you can focus on the next one. You might use the in-between time to write some reflections of what has gone before, then get yourself into the zone for the person you will be present for next. Answering emails and catching up on your to-do list does not give you the refreshment that you need. It might feel satisfying to tick things off the list, but it's not giving you the energy you need to be fully present.

Here are some questions to help you think about your time:

➡ How do you want to structure your weeks so you can get enough rest (let alone time to deal with the other aspects of running a business)?

➡ How do you want to structure your seasons? (For example, one of my coaching friends takes a sabbatical week every seven weeks.)

➡ How do you want to structure your years? How much holiday time is good for you and your energy levels, and how do you wish to spread it across the year?

➡ How will you spend your time off such that it is rejuvenating? (There is no one-size-fits-all answer to this question.)

➡ What are the signals that you need to take a break? That you have been overdoing it? Or that this cannot be business as usual? (There are some easy decisions here, like illness or death of a loved one or a pet, so that we can provide care and/or grieve. We must take a break and our thinkers will understand our need to reschedule.)

You also need to identify when your stress container is getting close to overflowing. For me, I know that I'm getting stressed when:

➡ I can't get to sleep, or when I wake up much too early or in the middle of the night and can't get back to sleep
➡ I feel the sense of running on a treadmill that's going faster and faster
➡ I snap at my husband
➡ I get annoyed with people behind their backs for things I'd normally let wash over me
➡ I can't focus
➡ I make stupid mistakes
➡ I feel helpless and hopeless.

– the list goes on.

These are my cues to stop and pay attention. Your cues will be unique to you, and it's worth naming them so that you'll recognise them when they happen. These are cues to do something about the stress, take a break and rearrange your diary.

Prevention is better than cure: look at the pauses you put in your hours, days, weeks and years to recharge before you need to do so. This pause is like defragging your computer. Clearing space. It will be a different pause for you compared with what it is for me.

My pause time between meetings consists of making a cup of tea or coffee, centring while the kettle boils, enjoying that drink while sitting, preferably outdoors, and doing nothing but savouring it. It usually involves dog cuddles.

I also build in weekly pauses, taking a morning or afternoon to step away from the computer and immerse myself in something creative, spend time with a friend, or explore a new part of the New Forest, where I live. And I'm starting monthly pauses too, reading weeks during the New Moon period when rest is most needed, according to Kirsty Gallagher (2020). I have to admit that I'm less disciplined at keeping these reading weeks free from client work; but like you, I'm a work-in-progress.

Then there's the yearly pause. I do this twice a year, once at my birthday and once between Christmas and New Year, reflecting on the year to date and planning for the next period. Holidays can be a great pause too, but we all know what it's like to push through until that time off, as we simply crash or get ill in our downtime if we do that. In among these pauses, we also need to pause for reflective practice and coaching supervision.

This layering of pauses, as Robert Poynton (2019) calls it, gives me higher yield than I would ever get if I pushed through and saw eight clients per day. When I say yield, I don't mean efficiency – I mean effectiveness, following Stephen Covey's (1999) lead. We can't be driven by the clock, he says; we must be driven by what's most important. What's important in coaching is being fully present with each thinker, no matter where they are in our day, so they can do their best thinking.

How will you be self-centred to look after yourself and your needs, so you're highly resourced for thinker-centred presence? How will you layer your pauses?

Retrieval practice 1

In *The Power of Teaching* (2019), Agarwal and Bain write that, for optimal learning, we must (among other things) stop and *retrieve* what we've read or heard. This is your opportunity to do just that. I know you're going to want to skip straight over this reflection piece, but by stopping for just a few minutes and writing down what your brain can retrieve, what you've read is more likely to stick and be more easily retrieved when you need it.

Here are some questions for you to answer in your journal:

➡ What do you recall from this chapter?
➡ What rings true to you?
➡ What do you see more clearly now?
➡ How does this feel in your body?
➡ What else do you sense?
➡ Which mindsets do you want to discard to make way for more transformational mindsets?
➡ What else did your parents or carers teach you that you could discard to be a more masterful coach?

Habit change commitment 1

It's time to commit to trying something different based on what has resonated with you. This template will help you to make *one* commitment to make *one* small change. When you're comfortable with that, you can make others.

➡ Instead of believing the voice in my head that says...
➡ Which leads me to do/say...
➡ I choose to believe...
➡ And will therefore do/say...
➡ My cue or reminder is...
➡ My immediate reward will be...

You may choose to share this commitment with a coaching buddy for more social accountability.

Now, stop reading and writing: go and experiment with what you have learned, before coming back for more mindset shifts in the rest of the book.

Chapter 2

Mindsets we learned at school that we need to discard to be a more masterful coach

School was obviously a place of learning. Besides subject matter, we learned all sorts of life and communication skills. Our teachers' expectations will have shaped the person we've become today. As you think about the messages that your teachers imparted, both spoken and unspoken, what did they teach you that you've needed to discard to be a more masterful coach?

▲ Shift 14

OLD MINDSET: Follow the rules
NEW MINDSET: Honour the thinker's needs

At school, unless we were a bit of a rebel, we learned to follow the rules. There were many: some were important to keep us safe, while others were perhaps more to meet our teachers' needs for control. Either way, there were rules.

Don't get me wrong, I believe in boundaries (see also Shift 2), and I'm actually quite the rule follower, getting annoyed with people who break societal and legal ones. But in coaching, rules can get in the way of our partnering with the thinker to meet their needs.

Coaches who come to mentor-coaching to get ready for their ICF Credential often get caught up with the PCC Markers as rules. Those rules feel stifling to their personalised coaching style: you must do X or Y, include these questions (such as the CONTRACT questions) to align with the rules of the PCC Markers.

Whether you're aligned with the ICF or a different coaching body or have just learned to coach, you might want to think about what 'rules' you're following, and whether you might do something different to honour the thinker's needs in the moment. We should stop thinking of the competencies and models as rules, as long as we're honouring the thinker's needs. CONTRACT (see also Shift 3) enables us to partner in understanding their needs in the first place.

Every coach will work in their unique style. We know this because in group mentor-coaching, when coaches are observing others coaching, they say that they might do something different at a certain point in time. This shows us that we can still bring our unique style into the coaching. We don't want to be cookie-cutter coaches who all do and say the same thing. That would be dull! A robot could do that (Isaacson 2021).

For me there are only three rules in coaching:

1. We trust the non-directive process, the thinker and ourselves.
2. We follow the thinker's agenda.

3. We partner to get to *new thinking*.

Let's take a moment to address any other objections you might have to the 'rule' of contracting at the start of each coaching session: I suspect you may have several objections (because I've heard them all from the coaches I have mentor-coached):

1. What if the thinker is eager to get going, and just gets into the content before we've had a chance to contract?
2. It feels so formulaic.
3. What if the thinker says something that really needs some exploration, but we haven't yet finished the contract?

My answers are as follows:

1. If the horse is out of the gate, corral it (sorry, the thinker) for a moment to contract by saying something along the lines of: 'Might we take a moment to figure out the end we have in mind for today's session?' or: 'Before we get into the detail, could we establish what it is you would like to walk away with today?'
2. It may feel formulaic the first few times you try something new, as you'll feel 'consciously incompetent' (Broadwell 1969) – but that's normal. Keep practising, and you'll find ways to use your own language that feels more authentic to you; you'll experience a shift in value that thinkers gain from their sessions.
3. Treat the contract like an accordion, where you take in air then play a little, then take in more air and play a little. You don't have to race through the contracting questions to get to the coaching. The contracting questions *are* the coaching; you'll recognise when there are emotions, words or patterns that need some enquiry in the midst of the contract. These enquiries will inform the shape of the contract and are vital. Ebb and flow with the contract.

♜ Shift 15

OLD MINDSET: Finish what you start
NEW MINDSET: Simply break the stalemate

Our teachers encouraged us to see things through to the end, submitting our complete homework on time. If we didn't do this, we'd get in trouble. That's my experience, anyway. What about yours? Society backs this up with introjections such as 'stick at it', 'don't be a quitter', 'don't give up', 'see it through'. This often drives us in later life to finish what we started.

For example, it has taken me many years not to finish reading a book that wasn't interesting or captivating. I felt compelled by the mindset instilled in me by my teachers to finish what I started. As a result, we coaches tend to want to finish everything off in a coaching session. Completeness is a draw. Getting to a conclusion is seductive. Finding solutions is irresistible (see also Shifts 15, 24, 31, 39, 45 and 51). A belief that we 'only' have so much time together and must finish everything in that time slot lures us to quicken the pace and get to the end (see also Shift 81).

As mentioned previously, as a coach you may fall into the trap of driving to the finish line, feeling as though it's your responsibility to cover everything the thinker said they wanted at the start – so you inadvertently push, lead and direct towards an outcome that meets their original session contract. That means you can miss or skip over exploration that could be useful to the thinker – and be more trans-formational for them.

You also might be assuming that you need to get as far as you can when you are together in coaching – that this thinker can't make any further progress on their own in between coaching sessions.

The thing is, once you've helped them to make some progress, that progress begets progress. Teresa Amabile and Steve Kramer (2011) found that any progress is good progress. Small wins count. People feel motivated to continue when they recognise they have made progress, even modestly. You're enabling them to break the stalemate in which they find themselves: that's your aim as a coach.

Tim Gallwey (2001) suggests that 'ideally, the end result of every coaching session is that the client leaves feeling more capable of mobility'.

Imagine a beaver dam. Metaphorically speaking, if we pull out one stick from that beaver dam, we allow a trickle of water through it. That trickle will start to push out more sticks, and as each stick floats away downstream, there's another gap for a little more water, then a little more until the water has washed away a whole section of the dam.

That's how we should approach coaching: as though our job in the session is to help the thinker to remove just one stick from the dam. If they can remove that one stick, they'll continue to remove obstacles after the coaching is over because progress begets progress.

Trust that once they have made any progress in the session, they'll continue outside of it without you. They may need you for the first stick, but they don't need you for the whole dam. You don't need to enable them to remove it all, or even half of it, for them to get huge value from the session.

You can let go of the need to finish what has been started in a coaching session. Also, let go of finishing what has been started in a programme of sessions. If the thinker hasn't quite achieved all of their coaching goals at the end of the contracted coaching sessions, don't automatically add one or two or three extra sessions to get them all the way. By this point, they may not need the coaching to keep moving towards that end point – if indeed that end point is still the same anyway.

To help them see what progress they're making, at the mid- and end-points, ask them questions such as:

➡ 'What is explicit now that wasn't explicit before?'
➡ 'What is evident now that wasn't evident before?'
➡ 'What is different for you now?'
➡ 'You said you wanted X; where are you now?'
➡ 'What progress have you made today towards your outcome of X?'

You can ask these same questions at the end of a coaching programme. Don't worry that they'll be disappointed about not getting to their final destination. If they feel that they've made progress, that will motivate them to keep making progress both between sessions and after a series of sessions is complete.

You can also ask them how they plan to continue their exploration outside of the session. For example:

➡ 'What are you taking away to explore further?'
➡ 'How do you want to continue this journey after the coaching session?'
➡ 'What would you like to experiment with as a result of today?'
➡ 'What did we not cover today that you still want to process?'
➡ 'Where will you take that?'

The same goes for the completion of the coaching programme:

➡ 'What are you still working on, as we come to the end of our work together?'
➡ 'How will you hold yourself accountable for making continued progress on that?'
➡ 'What resources can you draw on?'
➡ 'What support will you engage?'

Thinkers are adults: they can continue to make progress without you. Let's treat them as such, with the agency and capacity to keep making progress once their stalemate has been broken through. Witness their unfolding without needing an end result.

☑ Shift 16

OLD MINDSET: **More is more**
NEW MINDSET: **Less is more**

Many moons ago, when I went to Sunday school, my favourite time of year was when we were given an Easter project. We were tasked with telling a story from the Bible in our own words. I used to love putting my all into these projects, adding two dimensional depictions like lambs made of cotton wool, which got me extra marks for my project.

More was always more, and I was encouraged to go bigger and better each year by those extra marks. The problem was that this got me into a pattern of more is more. Once, I got stung by a wasp when my class was painting a joint mural for the wall, and had to leave the classroom. When I came back they were finished, but I wanted to add my stamp to the picture, so picked up a paintbrush and added more fluff to a cloud. That added extra didn't go down so well with my teacher.

In this case, less was definitely more.

In coaching, less is more too. But we seem to get drawn into this idea that to add value, we need to do more, say more, improve on what they've said. We end up getting in the way of the thinker's thinking by taking too much airspace.

For example, I notice how much airspace some coaches take with summarising what they've heard. It's not summarising at all; it's parroting back everything that the thinker has said. As one of the people I mentor-coach realised, she was doing this to buy herself time to formulate her next question – so it was for her benefit, not the thinker's. This isn't useful to the thinker because it stops them from thinking: they end up having to pay attention to us to tell us whether we've captured it all correctly or not. This is wasted time that could be spent on them moving further forwards in their thinking.

We need to refine our skills so that we can play back the golden nugget in what they just said rather than relaying all the sand and shingle (see also Shift 71).

Feed back the essence of what you heard *succinctly*, then get out so they can process. For example, 'I think I heard [one word] and [one word]. How does that resonate with you?'

Notice the emotion *succinctly*, then get out so they can process. 'I'm noticing the tear prick in your eye. What are the tears telling you?' (see also Shifts 35, 65 and 71).

Many coaches I observe also ask stacked questions, one after another, taking up more airspace. The first question was perfectly good; or if it wasn't, we can always ask the second one later. Some coaches feel the need to explain their question or preface it. Again, too much airspace.

There's no need to say: 'The question that is coming up for me is...' Just ask the question.

Or: 'I ask that because...' Just ask the question or make an observation about what you observe and see how they respond.

One question at a time.

Sometimes one-word questions are enough:

'So...?'
'And...?'
'[Insert word that they just used]?'

In fact, silence is often the best question, as they keep thinking (see also Shifts 30 and 34). One of my mentor-coachees who came from a media background came up with the idea of imagining a film clapperboard to remind him to 'cut'.

Less is more.

👥 Shift 17

OLD MINDSET: I must understand everything
NEW MINDSET: I don't need to understand, as long as the thinker does

At school and university, we were expected to listen to our teachers and lecturers so we could learn the information that they were trying to impart. I realise that not all learning is about listening. Indeed, we know from Knowles's (1975) adult learning theory that the best learning comes from self-discovery.

But much of our learning at school and university used the didactic approach of lectures – we listened to learn information. The aim was to *understand* what we were taught. If there was something we didn't understand, we were encouraged to ask questions to fill us in on the detail that didn't quite make sense to us, or to go and do some research in encyclopaedias or (these days) the Internet. Knowledge was our quest.

As coaches we ask questions, but for a quite different reason: not for our own understanding, but for the thinker's. Curiosity is important but not to fill us, the coach, in (see also Shifts 24 and 68). In coaching, you're not listening with a view to gaining information for yourself. You don't need to understand for yourself at all.

Recently, I listened to a Master Certified Coach who didn't ask any questions to learn information for herself. All her questions and observations were meant to be useful to the thinker, evoking new awareness. It matters not a jot whether you understand; it matters hugely that the thinker gains insight.

I've listened to a number of coaches as they coach where I notice this need to fill themselves in on the detail. I recognise this when the question is about the content of what has been said: picking up on one specific piece of content that isn't likely to add value for the thinker.

I also notice it when the coach says 'got it' after the thinker has spoken, as though they needed to get it to be able to support and challenge. That's one of the habits I'm trying to break myself.

Some coaches ask, once they've summarised: 'Did I understand that correctly?' or 'Did I get that right?' First, we don't need to understand it – the thinker does. Second, these questions make it all about us and our precision. Try replacing this with something like: 'How does that sound to you, as you hear it back?'

I also hear thinkers saying to coaches: 'Does that make sense to you?' That's their invitation to us to say that we understand. But it doesn't matter whether it makes sense to us. It matters whether it makes sense to them. A better response than 'yes' might be: 'What sense does it make to you?' or 'What is the meaning you make from that?'

It might seem counter-intuitive, but I don't need to understand what the thinkers are talking about. I have coached many people who talk in language that's unfamiliar to me, using jargon and acronyms from their industry or specialism of which I don't know the meaning. If I were to stop them with a question that enables me to understand something they already understand, I'd be taking time away from their ability to create new thinking.

I know one coach who has coached in English with a translator, but the translator only translated from English into the foreign language, not the other way. This coach has done this twice, once with a Russian speaker and once with a Hebrew speaker. She didn't understand anything that was said, but could still ask questions and make observations that moved the thinker's thinking forward.

I spoke with the coach in question, Jenny Bird (Master Certified Coach, coach supervisor and author), and asked her to elaborate on how this worked. She told me that she used what I call 'process questions' rather than 'content questions', also observations of what she was seeing. She contracted, then recontracted multiple times.

Underpinning these process questions was her trust in the process and the thinker, believing that they could (and would) do the thinking they needed to do in the session, and would go where they needed to go.

She also offered observations about the thinker's facial expressions, changes in pace and tone, body movement, for example: 'I notice you doing this [demonstrating the hand movement].' What is the meaning of that for you?' And when the hand movement shifted to something different, she noticed that too, imitating the difference with her own hands, but without words. The body movement in itself became a common language between them.

Jenny says that at the end of her session with the Russian thinker, the people watching the coaching demonstration asked her: 'Are you sure you don't speak Russian?' Her interventions, whether those were questions, observations or simply mimicking the hand gestures without words, seemed so on-point at every step of the way, that they couldn't believe that she hadn't understood the language. This is testament to the power of process questions and noticing.

Jenny and I have also both experimented with content-free coaching, whereby we ask a group of thinkers to each write down their answers to questions. Again, these are all process questions.

Let's differentiate between a content question and a process question.

A content question is one that picks up on something that the thinker has just said to explore that further. Claire Pedrick (2020) describes this as 'talking to the wavy people'. The wavy people are all of the pieces of content that a thinker talks about: they wave, try to engage and hook us into asking more about them. They want to be asked about; but often these questions don't lead to new thinking, instead to storytelling (see also Shift 4) or justification – in other words, known thinking.

Process questions are better. They keep you out of needing to understand and move the thinker towards new thinking, sensing and learning.

By now, you will recognise some of these process questions as contracting and recontracting questions (see also Shift 3):

Check-in: 'What would be most useful to think about today?'
Objective: 'What would you like to be different by the time we finish today?'
Necessity: 'What is it about this that is important to you right now?'
Time: 'What is your specific question for today's X minutes?'
Realisation: 'How will you know you have got what you need by the time we wrap up today?'
Agenda: 'What is your sense of what we need to cover today to get to your outcome?'

Co-creation: 'How would you like us to work together today?' 'How much challenge are you up for?' 'May I have permission to interrupt in service of new thinking?'
Their Agenda: 'Where shall we start?'

You can see that there's not an ounce of content in any of these questions. They could be asked of anyone about anything. Recontracting might sound like:

➡ 'What is explicit now that wasn't explicit before?'
➡ 'You said you wanted X; where are you now?'
➡ 'What have you noticed so far?'

Followed by:

➡ 'Where would you like to go next?'
➡ 'We have X minutes; what would be most useful?'
➡ 'Where does that take your thinking next?'

If the thinker seems to have gone off on a tangent in their goal for the session, you might ask:

➡ 'At the beginning you said you wanted X, and we now seem to be talking about Y. What's the connection?'
➡ 'Do we need to shift our focus or go back to X?'

If they want to cover Y, you might want to use the CONTRACT questions again, lightly.

There are so many other places throughout a session where you can use process rather than content questions, nudging them forwards as you listen with the questions outlined previously, such as:

'So...?'
'And...?'
'What else?'
'And the headlines are...?'

Or when the thinker asks themselves a question... 'Go on, then.' Or say the question back to them. You'll likely notice they squirm as they realise that they can't brush off that question, but it's bound to be powerful as it is theirs.

'As you hear yourself, what you do hear yourself saying?'

There's no content in any of those questions.

Checking in as you explore together continues the theme of process questions:

➡ 'Where are we?'
➡ 'What next?'
➡ 'Is this useful?'
➡ 'How are we doing in moving you towards new thinking?'
➡ 'What do we need to do differently together to get you to new thinking?'
➡ 'What are you noticing?'

Again, there's no content in any of these questions.

Process questions come up again as we CLOSE the session:

Consolidation: 'We have X minutes left. You said you wanted X today... what progress have you made towards that?' 'What experiments are you committing to after the session that will continue your progress?'
Learning: 'What are you hoping to learn from your experiments?' 'What have you learned about yourself today that you can apply in this situation and beyond?'
Obstacles: 'What might get in your way?'
Support: 'How will you hold yourself accountable?' 'What support mechanisms might you put in place?' 'What internal and external resources can you draw on?'
End: 'On that note, is that enough for today?'

As we haven't looked at CLOSE yet, let's delve deeper to understand the rationale behind each question, as we did with CONTRACT in Shift 3:

Consolidation: 'We have X minutes left. You said you wanted X today... what progress have you made towards that?'
'Coach invites or allows the client to explore progress toward what the client wanted to accomplish in the session' (PCC Marker 8.1).

➡ First, we are signposting time again here, making sure that we are *both* in the know about where we are in the session and how much time we have available to us.

➡ We are also asking them to acknowledge their progress, recognising that progress begets progress after the session (see also Shift 15).

➡ We could also ask: 'What difference will this progress make to you?'

'What experiments are you committing to after the session that will continue your progress?'
'Coach partners with the client to design post-session thinking, reflection or action' (PCC Marker 8.5).

➡ I use the word experiment here because people find it less threatening than: 'What are you going to *do*?' The 'doing' word suggests a long-term commitment, whereas experiment suggests more trial and error, more testing and tweaking, more one small step at a time with the ability to change direction than one massive step.

➡ We are presupposing that they'll continue with their progress. We trust they will make progress, which is more likely to lead them to make even more progress (Rosenthal and Jacobson 1968).

➡ Notice that PCC Marker 8.5 also covers post-session thinking or reflection. Action or experimentation is not always applicable, so an alternative might be: 'What further reflection will you engage in as a result of your thinking today?'

Learning: 'What are you hoping to learn from your experiments?'
'Coach invites the client to consider how they will use new learning from this coaching session' (PCC Marker 8.4).
'What have you learned about yourself today that you can apply in this situation and beyond?'
'Coach invites the client to state or explore the client's learning in this session about themself' (PCC Marker 8.2).

➡ 'This situation and beyond' enables the thinker to extrapolate the learning to apply to other situations alongside the one they brought to coaching.

➡ This broadens out the applicability of their learning, and will lead to greater change than they might have foreseen originally.

Obstacles: 'What might get in your way?'
'Coach partners with the client to consider how to move forward, including resources, support or potential barriers' (PCC Marker 8.6).

➡ You may be thinking it's a bit late to be asking about what's getting in their way, but this question is specifically about what might get in the way of them carrying out their experiments or post-session reflections.
➡ It's not a rehash of the original obstacles that were in their way at the start of the session as they have moved beyond those by now.

Support: 'How will you hold yourself accountable?'
'Coach partners with the client to design the best methods of accountability for themself' (PCC Marker 8.7).

➡ Note that this is about how the thinker will hold themselves accountable, not you as the coach. You need to help them build their own muscles in this arena, so they can do this for themselves when you're no longer with them.
➡ They may ask you to be an accountability partner – if that's OK with you, you can agree; but this shouldn't be the first offer on the table.
➡ Better if they can find someone in their own network who can act as an accountability buddy, as that person will be there in the long run and you will not.

'What support mechanisms might you put in place?'
'Coach partners with the client to consider how to move forward, including resources, support or potential barriers' (PCC Marker 8.6).

➡ This enables the thinker to find some scaffolding to remind them of their experiments or reflective practice.
➡ Don't presume to know what good support mechanisms might be for them. I've lost count of the number of times I've been surprised at the answer to this question, as a thinker came up with something I'd never have thought of personally.

'What internal and external resources can you draw on?'
'Coach partners with the client to consider how to move forward, including resources, support or potential barriers' (PCC Marker 8.6).

➡ Internal resources may be their own inner wisdom, so I sometimes also ask: 'What words of wisdom do you have for yourself, as we close this session?' or 'What aspects of you would you like to celebrate as we close?'

End: 'On that note, is that enough for today?'
'Coach partners with the client on how they want to complete this session' (PCC Marker 8.9).

➡ Coaches often ask me whether this question might lead to a reopening of another topic for discussion. It's unlikely, if you have signposted time throughout and recontracted where it felt necessary.

➡ Occasionally, you'll experience what therapists call a 'door-handle moment' or an 'exit line' (Gabbard 1982), when the thinker says something as they leave that seems as if it might have been the most important thing for them to cover. It's akin to a cliff-hanger. They're relieved to have said it, even if they didn't bring it into the conversation.

➡ You might be tempted to rescue at this point, but assuming they haven't expressed a danger to themselves or others, hold back and simply ask: 'Where do you feel safe enough to continue to think about that?'

In this Shift, I've highlighted process questions as an alternative to content questions. At every stage, your role as coach is to enable *the thinker* to understand, not you.

This is the power of process questions that aren't taking you both back into the story, or gathering information to fill you in; rather, moving the thinker forwards in their own knowing, understanding and potential action.

 # Shift 18

In my school, my teachers often encouraged us to keep quiet unless we were asked to contribute. They wanted us to keep our heads down, listen, give them space to teach. It's understandable (although the antithesis of modern methods of fostering learning), as they have content to impart that they want all of the class to hear and take in. Does this sound familiar to you?

There's such a fine line in coaching between allowing the thinker to think out loud – in service of new thinking, not old story – and adding value through what we see and hear. If we listen endlessly, we might be in what Blakey and Day (2012) call the 'cosy corner'. As identified previously, this is a cosy chat and not particularly challenging. Our mindset shouldn't be just to do this, but to listen and then highlight the essence, or notice the emotions, patterns or inconsistencies.

When we say what we see or hear, succinctly and without selling it, the thinker may realise something they hadn't realised previously, even if it was something they said or did.

If you read the ICF PCC Markers for Listens Actively below, you will understand how this shows up:

➡ 'Coach enquires about or explores the words the client uses' (PCC Marker 6.2)
➡ 'Coach enquires about or explores the client's emotions' (PCC Marker 6.3)
➡ 'Coach explores the client's energy shifts, non-verbal cues or other behaviours' (PCC Marker 6.4)
➡ 'Coach *succinctly* reflects or summarises what the client communicated to ensure the *client's* clarity and understanding' (emphasis added; PCC Marker 6.7)

As you can see from these Markers, it isn't enough to say what you see or hear without asking what the thinker notices about that. For example:

➡ '[Whatever word they just used that merits further exploration]?'
➡ 'You've used the word 'X' multiple times. What is important to you about that?'
➡ 'I heard you say X and Y are important to you. How do you make sense of that?' The statement is the saying what you heard; the question is enabling the thinker to explore its meaning to them.
➡ 'You said you are angry, and I can hear that. What other emotions are going on for you that could give you some insights?'
➡ 'I noticed that your facial expression changed then. What's that about?' The statement is the saying what you see (without a diagnosis of what that might mean), the question is enabling the thinker to explore its meaning to them.
➡ 'What's that giggle/sigh/tear about?'

These enquiries and explorations are what make the listening active rather than passive: the observation *and* the enquiries or exploration. They also evoke awareness, in particular PCC Marker 7.5: 'Coach shares – with no attachment – observations, intuitions, comments, thoughts or feelings, and invites the client's exploration through verbal or tonal invitation'. We also see this in Trust and Safety PCC Marker 4.4: 'Coach partners with the client by inviting the client to respond in any way to the coach's contributions and accepts the client's response.'

Doing so without attachment, accepting the client's response, means that you let go of it if it doesn't land. If the thinker says it's not anger (for example) but something else, that's new learning for them, and you should go where they go as a result of the observation.

Saying what you see, hear or sense is one of your superpowers as a coach, and you must overcome the tendency to listen ad infinitum.

🦋 Shift 19

OLD MINDSET: There's a right answer for everything

NEW MINDSET: Whatever emerges, emerges

At school, we learn the right answers. There are plenty of domains where there's only one right answer. A maths equation only has one right answer (albeit you can get partial credit for showing your working). Rock formations have certain names that we must remember in geology. In law, there are cases that we must be able to recall. Granted, there's not always one right answer. In the English language, for example, we can develop our own writing style. In exam questions, we're invited to discuss a provocative statement which could have multiple interpretations. But mostly, my memories of school are about getting things right.

And because it's been instilled in us, it's hard to let go of that. I see many coaches leading thinkers towards an answer that the coach sees as *the* (or maybe *a*) 'right' answer. The problem with this is that in coaching, there's rarely one right answer. It happens occasionally when an internal coach notices that the person they're coaching could benefit from knowing about a certain internal policy, for example.

That still doesn't necessarily provide the one right answer, but as Peter Hawkins and Nick Smith (2013) say: 'The work of the learning enabler is never to know better, and never to know first but to create the enabling conditions.' I've heard Peter say verbally in addition, 'to never withhold information that could be useful'. That is, pointing the thinker towards the policy, for example, to check it out themselves and decide how to implement it in their situation.

The times where a right answer is there for the taking are rare. If it were that obvious, the thinker would have discovered it by now. They wouldn't need coaching – they could look it up on the Internet! The answer that's most useful to each thinker will be the one that suits their personality, context, values, stakeholders, situation and life stage – the matrix goes on. The answer that worked for us or for an earlier thinker isn't going to be a perfect match for this current person's matrix. They're unique, and their matrix makes them so. That means the answer will be unique to them.

Let go of there being one (right) answer. I put 'right' in parentheses here, because even when a thinker comes to some conclusion for themselves, they may still need to experiment and tinker with it until it becomes the best-fit answer for them, or even throw it out completely and start afresh. There may be some trial and error involved, as the best-fit answer may be elusive.

Believing in our core that there is a best-fit answer for this person, that is different from the best-fit answer for the next person, is quite a shift. I hear coaches talking about this as though they believe it, yet their coaching contradicts this belief: they ask leading questions, or give advice disguised as a question.

Listen to recordings of your coaching, alone or with a mentor-coach, to establish which belief you're living:

➡ Are you asking questions from a place of not knowing?
➡ Is your mind clear of suggestions?
➡ Or are you leading the thinker to solutions that have worked for you or others in the past?

That will give you a hint about your true belief here. Embrace the belief that whatever emerges, emerges. That belief shows up in asking more process, and fewer content, questions. (Refer back to Shift 17 for ideas of process questions.) Also, more 'who'-based questions, such as:

➡ 'What is the [their feeling] you are being with that we need to explore?'
➡ 'How are you talking to yourself when you use the word [their word]?'
➡ 'What is the connection between [their word] and [their word] that we need to explore here together?'
➡ 'What is the significance of [their word], and how might it connect with what you're looking for in this session?'
➡ 'What is it about [their word] that blocks your vision?'
➡ 'How are you missing yourself?'
➡ 'What beliefs are you crafting that could sustain you?'
➡ 'What are you believing that stops you?'
➡ 'What's your relationship to [their word]?'

This is coaching the person not the problem, as Marion Franklin (2019) and Marcia Reynolds (2020) call it.

Please don't treat these as a list of powerful questions to plug in wherever and whenever. Questions lose their potency if they're plugged and played. Find questions that work in the moment for the thinker with whom you are working right now, given where they are.

We'll come back to these kinds of questions when we explore going deeper to go further (see also Shifts 46 and 63).

 # Shift 20

OLD MINDSET: **If it's not measurable, it's not to be trusted**
NEW MINDSET: **Felt sense is wisdom**

Scientists and mathematicians measure the world. There's no room for intuition or bodily sensing in their world. I'm making a generalisation here of course, but when we hear, over and over again, questions such as: 'How do you measure that?', 'How do you know?', 'What are the facts?', intuition and felt sense tend to get lost.

One of the people I interviewed noticed that this came from his father and school: that it had really shaped his adult life, and needed therapeutic work to disrupt and replace it for him to be free both to access his intuition and bodily senses and enable thinkers to do the same.

As coaches, that is something we need to build back again. First, because the answers in coaching are rarely factual and logical – if they were, we wouldn't need coaching; we could look it up on the Internet! You've heard me say that before, and it bears repeating. Second, because there's so much data in our heart, gut and body in general that may be different to what is in our head.

As coaches we need to access our heart, gut and body to be able to ask questions from a different perspective or offer observations from a different place, and we need to enable thinkers to access wisdom from different sources other than their rational head.

What does that sound like? Questions might be:

➡ 'How does your gut feel?' then: 'What does that say to you?'
➡ 'What's going on in your heart?' then: 'What does that offer to you?'
➡ 'Where do you feel that in your body?' then: 'What is the message in that for you?'

We might also use metaphors to frame our questions:

➡ 'If this were a journey, what would you notice on that journey?'
➡ 'If this were a tree, what would the tree be saying?'
➡ 'What is a metaphor that's coming up for you here that could shed some light on the subject?'
➡ 'I notice a metaphor here. May I share it with you to see what it might offer to you?'

By the way, these aren't questions that will work anytime, anyplace or anywhere. They need to be created in the moment, based on what you've heard and seen. These are simply examples to get the gist by using these other parts of the body–brain – those which are not all in our heads.

▣ Shift 21

OLD MINDSET: Take copious notes
NEW MINDSET: Be present and let your memory work for you

As students from school through to college then university, we were encouraged to take notes, the theory being that this would help us to remember what we were taught. That may have worked for you, or it may not. Often I hear coaches say: 'I have to write it down, otherwise I'll forget it.' Perhaps this comes from that history, or perhaps coaches don't trust themselves enough. There's an implication that we need to remember it, and there's no other way of remembering.

When the belief that note-taking is essential is carried into coaching without a second thought, it can get in the way. How? By stopping us from being fully present. If we're writing notes, we often miss what the thinker is actually saying. We miss their facial expressions (if we are face-to-face or screen-to-screen). We likely miss their tone of voice, pitch, pace, etc. – *how* they said it – because we are too busy trying to capture the details of *what* they said. There's so much data in how they say things. And if you're writing with your head down, you'll miss those data points, cutting off a plethora of useful reflections.

The thinker is also missing your full engagement, and your trust quotient might decrease as a result. Moreover, when you take notes, the thinker will often wait for you to finish writing, seeing you as the owner of their key information. They're so polite that they want to give you a chance to catch up, as though this is your time, not theirs. But it is their valuable thinking time, and you're wasting it as they stop in their tracks to let you catch up. It can also look as though you're writing notes to diagnose their issue and come out with some brilliant answer to their problem. This, too, stops them from thinking for themselves.

If you're writing, how can you be fully present: the most important of all the coaching competencies, and fully conscious to their thinking? How can you empower them to do their best thinking?

It's time to put the pen down, stop multitasking and start single-tasking – paying attention in the round.

You might argue with me that you need to remember what they've said. I would counter: for what purpose, to be able to recount it back to them? In answer to that, I encourage you to look at Shifts 16 and 71 on playing back the highlights, the essence, not the executive summary. Or asking them to summarise what they now know or sense and what difference knowing that makes to them.

Is it to be able to recall next time what you talked about in this session? They will have moved on since the last session, so why hold on to that piece of history? Maybe they've asked you to hold them to account for making progress – OK, so just write down what they want to be held accountable for (if you think that's the coach's role, which I personally think is infantilising; but that's a different story, as highlighted in Shift 70).

Is it to be able to remember their desired outcome for this session? Yes, I can buy that argument, and I do write down what their question is for the session and how they will know they have got that by the time we finish the session together. That way, I can use their words to recontract part-way through, and ask what progress they've made towards that at the end.

But that's it. That's all that I write.

This is their stuff, for which they are responsible. If they want to write notes, that's their prerogative. If they don't want to write notes because it gets in the way of their thinking, they can record the session as a way of keeping tabs on what they said. I've collaborated with several thinkers who have availed themselves of this option. That's one more reason, alongside all the others we've mentioned, why *you* don't need to keep tabs.

Shift 22

OLD MINDSET: Show the working out

NEW MINDSET: Keep your questions pithy without selling them

Did your maths teacher tell you to always show your working? I have such a vivid memory of that because I knew it could get me marks, even if I got the final answer wrong (which I did quite often, maths not being my strong suit). It was absolutely the right lesson to learn back then, in that context.

But it doesn't work for coaching. It gets in the way when we explain how we landed on the question we're about to ask. It takes up time – the thinker's thinking time – when we prattle on about all the connections we're making. Not only that, but it also suggests they might not make those connections for themselves if we were to ask them the question: 'What's the connection for you between X and Y?' Their connection is way more significant to them than ours.

It's unnecessary to explain our choice of question. When I'm observing coaches, I see too many prefixes to questions – and too many suffixes. The question loses its potency. Prefixes such as: 'May I ask you a question…', 'I'm curious…' or a long-winded summary of what they have just said.

And suffixes such as asking the question a second time, using different words or explaining the question.

Keep your questions pithy. Don't sell them. Just ask them and let them land. Don't fill the silence around them. Allow the thinker to use the silence to process the question. Mary Budd Rowe (1972) found that students need up to five seconds of silence to hear the question, process it and come to an answer. That's when it's a factual answer, so a thinker needs longer to ponder when they're not retrieving a fact from their memory bank, but new thinking instead. So don't suck out the silence by adding more unnecessary fluff.

Pithy might sound like:

➡ 'What is the meaning of [their word] to you?'

➡ 'What are you noticing?'

➡ 'Earlier you said X, and now you have said Y; what is the connection between those for you?'

Short and sweet. And robust!

◈ Shift 23

OLD MINDSET: Every subject is important
NEW MINDSET: Thinkers decide which avenue(s) to explore

I hear some coaches say they need lots of time to cover everything that the thinker brings to the coaching. Their coaching sessions are long, so they can delve into every nook and cranny. I'm not entirely sure where this comes from: perhaps it's a need for completeness. Perhaps it's something from school around spending equal time on each subject.

The thing is, our role is not to make sure that everything is ticked and tied, or to explore every angle. Our role is to enable the thinker to decide where they go next.

PCC Marker 5.5 reads: 'Coach partners with the client by supporting the client to choose what happens in this session' – which means that we are not deciding that for them. The thinker gets to decide what's important to cover in the session, and what to leave untouched. They decide on the direction. They do this by having you, the coach, ask something along the lines of: 'Given what you sense now, where do we need to explore next?' or 'What would give you the most value in our remaining X minutes?'.

I'm not saying that you let them off the hook from looking at the hard stuff. As I write about in Shifts 5, 29 and 53, we *do* ask the tough questions, but in the context of what they say they want to work on. If we have high trust between us, they can still say they don't want to go wherever our challenge might take them. They need to feel that they can push back when something more important is revealing itself to them.

You can achieve a lot in a short space of time, even 20–30 minutes. That's anathema to some coaches but if you follow the thinker's agenda, it's surprising how far they can go – if you believe in the potential of time rather than its limitations (see also Shift 81). And if they did list out some other aspects to cover that weren't covered due to time or their own capacity to take any more on, you can simply ask: 'Where will you process the rest?' – giving them credit for being able to do that without you.

⚖ Shift 24

OLD MINDSET: Teachers hold the truth
NEW MINDSET: Be curious about multiple truths

At school, we looked up to our teachers (I did, anyway). They were the font of all knowledge, at least in their subject, if not beyond. They knew everything. They held the truth, the one right answer. Ours was not to question that. (OK, so this was me – 'little Miss Goody Two-shoes', teacher's pet.) You may not have looked up to your teachers in the same way, unquestioningly, but hopefully you get the point. Even if in some small way you were influenced by this belief, you may have carried forward with you the belief that there's just one truth, one way of doing things – the expert way, your way.

That may creep into your coaching, where you give solutions perhaps disguised as questions, perhaps not. Questions such as:

➡ 'Have you thought of...?'
➡ 'Have you tried...?'
➡ 'How about you...?'

Or perhaps more directive:

➡ 'Here's what I/another thinker did in your situation...'

All of these come from a place of believing that there's only one right answer – the one that you know. But there may be (and usually are) multiple answers, stemming from multiple truths:

➡ my truth is not your truth is not another person's truth
➡ my beliefs are not your beliefs are not another person's beliefs
➡ my personality is not your personality is not another person's personality
➡ my history is not your history is not another person's history

– and so on.

The way forward comes from a person's own truth, beliefs, values, personality and history, etc., so your role as coach is to be curious on the thinker's behalf, to enable them to uncover their own truths – and their own adjustable truths, if that serves them better. Not to become your truths, but to become their own new truths.

In fact, the thinker may hold contradictory truths, which are worth exploring to see what meaning they make of the contradictions. For example: 'I heard you say X, now I am hearing Y; what is the relationship of those to each other?'

Not because you see something different, but to enable them to see, feel or notice something useful to them. And not to prove that you have the answers, but to enable them to touch, taste, smell, feel or know their own answers.

This is curiosity on their behalf, not to fill you in on information. Curiosity that gets to new thinking, not going over old ground (see also Shifts 17 and 68).

 # Shift 25

OLD MINDSET: Offer praise such as 'great', 'interesting', 'excellent'
NEW MINDSET: Offer positive acknowledgement of who they are

Somewhere along the line we have learned to say 'great' or 'excellent' in response to another person's musings. Or we say: 'That's interesting,' or even 'yes' or 'yeah' during their sentences to encourage them to keep going. These are all judgements, albeit positive ones.

You may think that is OK because they are positive, but what if you don't say, 'That's interesting,' the next time they say something they think is interesting? Will that encourage them to say things for your sake rather than for their learning and new thinking, or will they feel deflated that they didn't get the praise? And what if they hear these as confirmation that their idea is a good one, and they should go forth and do it?

I notice that thinkers often believe that the coach came up with the idea if we judge them in this way. This is the opposite of our intention, which is to encourage them to own their own ideas.

Besides which, something may not be positive to them.

Take this story of a recovering cancer survivor who went to her first Zumba class post-illness. The person she was recounting this to told her how amazing it was that she had managed her first Zumba class.

But she said it was awful, as no one recognised her without her long hair. The praise was uncalled-for, and got in the way of the person describing her own feelings about the situation.

We like to be positive though, so with what do we replace the praise? Acknowledgement of who the thinker is being in the moment. 'Acknowledgment recognises the inner character of the person it is addressed to,' wrote Whitworth et al. in *Co-active Coaching* (1998). Such acknowledgement might recognise one of the thinker's values. Schools have moved towards recognising effort, for example, not just achievement.

In coaching, an example might be something like: 'I hear your desire to work this out for yourself, and you have done exactly that in this session.' (The context here was that they felt they couldn't do this thinking alone, yet were self-coaching for much of the session.)

Another example might be:

'From what you're saying, you took a significant risk in instigating that conversation – congratulations. I know you wanted to be yourself while also standing up for what you know to be true, and I hear that you did just that. I notice how differently you show up today compared to three months ago, demonstrating X, Y and Z.'

I've noticed that the acknowledgements that have the most impact are the ones where the thinker is minimising themselves and not accessing the strength that they're demonstrating, so they need to hear it from an external source.

I'm working with one person, for example, who downplays the risks he has taken, the courage it took to do something, the fear he had to overcome, or the tenacity that something took.

By my acknowledging the risks, courage, fear or tenacity, he's starting to believe in himself and his capacity to continue to be courageous.

This acknowledgement will have a much greater impact on the thinker and their belief in themselves, compared with positive judgements in the form of praise which, counter-intuitively, can undermine their belief in themselves and their own ideas instead (see also Shift 7).

🌱 Shift 26

OLD MINDSET: Fixed mindset
NEW MINDSET: Growth mindset

According to the coaches I interviewed, school systems around the world historically have perpetuated – and perhaps still do – a fixed mindset in their learners. In the UK, at every step of the way we measure, test, assess, evaluate, score and chart schools on a 'leader board'. This often leads to what Carol Dweck (2017) calls a 'fixed mindset'.

According to Dweck, this fixed mindset limits us to learning only what we need to pass exams, or get the next promotion. Failure at any stage of the ongoing ladder of assessments makes us believe we've reached the limit of our abilities or that we're either good at something or not, so there would be no point in trying to learn or grow into it, and we might just as well give up when we get frustrated.

We stick to what we know.

As coaches, our job is to tap into the growth mindset, both for ourselves and for the thinkers with whom we partner. Those with a growth mindset, says Dweck, 'understand that their talents and abilities can be developed through effort…, and persistence'. Pay attention to your own fixed or growth mindset, being a role model for thinkers.

Those with a growth mindset are more likely to:

➡ embrace lifelong learning
➡ believe intelligence can be improved
➡ put in more effort to learn
➡ believe effort leads to mastery
➡ believe failures are just temporary setbacks
➡ view feedback as a source of information
➡ willingly embrace challenges
➡ view others' success as a source of inspiration, rather than comparison with their own failings
➡ view feedback as an opportunity to learn.

When we first learn to coach, many of us think we've been coaching for years and the training we've embarked on is simply brushing up on what we're already good at doing. Little do we realise how much of our earlier practice we need to discard before we can relearn to be a more masterful coach. When we make mistakes in our initial practice, we need to look on those as an opportunity to grow. We need to be challenged from the outside in the form of constructive feedback from experienced coaches to help us grow. Effort and attitude are what will determine our abilities as a coach.

I notice how many coaches start to doubt themselves as they come out of their training. 'Am I good enough?' they start to ask themselves. Inept feedback can leave them raw. Lack of feedback can leave them in a vacuum. They've been learning in a bit of a cocoon and now, as they build their coaching practice, they no longer have the security of the learning environment.

It's essential to find a mentor-coach who can give evidence-based feedback that builds your confidence in your own strengths, as well as helps you to see where you could sharpen up for the benefit of the thinker. Also of benefit is a coaching triad with whom to practice, although be sure to work with people who are at least as good as you – if not better – so that the feedback stretches you out of your comfort zone.

I suggest you use the following to guide your feedback to each other, so that it's evidence-based rather than subjective. This is an extract from my earlier book, *Mentor Coaching: A Practical Guide* (2020). Feedback should:

➡ be objective and factual: What did you see?, What did you hear?
➡ be observations of behaviour, particularly where there's a pattern, without interpretation, evaluation or judgement
➡ be succinct, without selling our point
➡ be supportive and challenging: a strength and a stretch
➡ be 'Adult–Adult', not 'Parent–Child' (Berne 1964)
➡ not minimise the stretch feedback (for example, 'this is just a little thing')
➡ focus on the coach, not the thinker.

People with a fixed mindset tend not to like making mistakes, but it's in reflection on our mistakes that we gain the most learning.

Coaches who listen to recordings of their coaching with me get more learning from the sessions that didn't go so well, than from those that did.

Of course, I'm not encouraging you to make mistakes on purpose in coaching. But you will; we all do. I don't know a single Master Certified Coach who thinks they complete a perfect coaching session, ever. We should bring our best selves to the coaching, but not our perfectionist selves. Treat every session like an experiment, a place to be curious, untethered by rules (see also Shifts 14, 28, 42 and 69).

Bring your growth mindset, not your fixed one.

🐾 Shift 27

OLD MINDSET: Always try your hardest
NEW MINDSET: Being easeful leads to better coaching

This one might sound familiar. Our parents or carers may well have taught us to try our hardest (see also Shift 3). Our teachers encouraged the same trait, urging us to give our utmost in all situations, to persist in difficult situations. This has its benefits, of course, otherwise we wouldn't be invited to try so hard. But there are significant downsides when we take all the responsibility, and we could eventually burn out.

In Shift 3, I wrote about getting thinkers to do the hard work of thinking. Here, I focus on you, the coach, being easeful.

As Kim Morgan (2019) wrote in *The Coach's Survival Guide*:

> If you are in a hurry to see transformation in your clients, you will unconsciously or perhaps even consciously, communicate this to them. This will put pressure on them and may make them feel that they are letting you down by not changing quickly enough. Alternatively, it may cause them to become resistant to you and therefore to changing. Working with ease, not urgency is essential in building the coaching relationship and creating the right conditions for your client to feel safe enough to explore new thoughts and behaviours.

Wilfred Bion (1967) suggests going into a session without memory or desire (see also Shift 40): this is what I mean by easeful. Letting go of the need to remember, know, achieve or understand. If you approach coaching in this way, you will feel less pressure to be perfect and complete (see also Shifts 15, 23 and 61). Less pressure to find the 'right' answers (see also Shifts 19 and 24).

Why is this better than trying hard? Because this is the thinker's life, not yours. But also because you can support and challenge them better from this place of ease, than you can from a place of pressure that you place on yourself when you try hard.

Let's take a moment to step back and reflect on drivers, as defined by Kahler (1975). Alongside 'Try hard', there are 'Be Perfect', 'Hurry Up', 'Please People' and 'Be Strong'. As Julie Hay (2009) states:

> [These drivers or working styles] are subconscious attempts by us to behave in ways that will gain us the recognition we need from others; they are also programmed responses to the messages we carry in our heads from important people in the past.

How do we let go of the need to try hard when it's so ingrained in us? Klein (1992) suggested it stems from fear of both failure and success. If you recognise that you try hard, the counter-encouragement is to tell yourself that it's OK to be yourself, and to just be.

Approach a session believing that there's no need to know, understand, have the answers, get to a rounded-out solution or achieve.

Get comfortable with:

➡ not knowing the/an answer, where the session is going or the perfect question
➡ progress that isn't necessarily the full solution
➡ the thinker with whom you're partnering taking the lead and doing the hard graft.

But how do you create ease before you enter a session? And how do you decompress afterwards, to let go of any residual unease?

What are your sources of ease? Meditation, centring, reflection, walking, music that slows your heartbeat? These are all slowing-down mechanisms. Some of you may want to rev up to find ease in your body through dancing, loud music, running or other movement. You'll know what works best for you, and only you can build it into your coaching entry and exit time.

These are transition times and we know as coaches, from the work of William Bridges (2004), that we need to treat transitions wisely.

If you are wearing a different hat before the coaching, be sure to consciously change it. For example, from mum (otherwise you might show up as a parent to the thinker), from consultant, mentor, teacher or any other role (so that you don't inadvertently play those roles rather than coach). Imagine that you are disrobing at the coaching door, and putting on a different cloak.

Make this a conscious, easeful transition: making a good ending, so you can begin the coaching well.

Retrieval practice 2

This is your opportunity to stop and reflect on what you've read, to retrieve what you remember in service of your long-term memory. You might be tempted to skip straight over this reflection piece, but by stopping for just a few minutes and writing down what your brain can retrieve, what you've read is more likely to stick and more easily retrieved when you need it.

Here are some questions for you to write the answers to:

➡ What do you recall from this chapter?
➡ What rings true to you?
➡ What do you see more clearly now?
➡ How does this feel in your body?
➡ What else do you sense?
➡ Which mindsets do you want to discard to make way for more transformational mindsets?
➡ What else did your teachers teach you that you could discard to be a more masterful coach?

Habit change commitment 2

It's time to commit to trying something different, based on what has resonated with you. This template will help you to make *one* commitment to make *one* small change. When you're comfortable with that, you can make another and another.

➡ Instead of believing the voice in my head that says...
➡ Which leads me to do/say...
➡ I choose to believe...
➡ And will therefore do/say...
➡ My cue or reminder is...
➡ My immediate reward will be...

You may choose to share this commitment with a coaching buddy for more social accountability.

Now, stop reading and writing: go and experiment with what you have learned, before coming back for more mindset shifts in the rest of the book.

Chapter 3

Mindsets we learned from our peers that we need to discard to be a more masterful coach

Peer pressure means that we learned to do, say or wear things that would enable us to fit in with our group. It's normal to want to be part of a tribe – whichever one we pick – so that we feel human connection and belonging (Baumeister and Leary 1995). Those expectations of our peers will have shaped the person we are today.

As you think about the messages that your peers imparted, both spoken and unspoken, and both from school days and more recently, what did they teach you that you have needed to discard to be a more masterful coach?

 # Shift 28

OLD MINDSET: Do what it takes to fit in
NEW MINDSET: Be yourself

At the big-picture level, the message from peers is that we need to fit in with the norms of the group, adhere to its values, believe what it believes and use language that's part of its vernacular. This is a message we continue to hear at work: fit through the cardboard cut-out of 'what good looks like' if you want to get on around here.

It's no wonder that new coaches want to fit in, adhere to 'the rules', live up to the expectations of their training school, mentor-coach or supervisor, to be in with the in-crowd. It's part of belonging. Attachment theory, as outlined by John Bowlby (1988), gives us insights into belonging. Creating an emotional or physical attachment to another human (usually a caregiver) allows us to feel safe and stable enough to take risks, move out of our comfort zone, stretch ourselves and grow.

Despite our desire to fit in, we each have such a rich tapestry of history behind us that makes us all unique as coaches. Each coach will bring something different to coaching because of who they are. That means that although (I hope) you will align yourself with a coaching body such as the ICF and its code of ethics, you won't become a cookie-cutter coach. And although each coaching body has its own set of competencies that define best practice, you will bring those competencies to life in your own unique way.

I do use the ICF competencies to guide me and how I show up as a coach, but I know that I'm quite different from the next coach and the next coach and the next, and I don't hide that uniqueness under a bushel. In fact, I notice that coaches often choose a niche that's based on their own history, battles and joy.

For example, coaching for introverts from an introvert herself; a wellbeing coach, based on personal experience of burnout; coaching for neurodivergent thinkers from a neurodivergent coach;

leadership coaching, where the coach has seen a gap in the people development side of leadership in organisations (that one is me!). That makes sense.

Be the coach you were shaped to be (although don't stop reshaping yourself, per all of the marginal gains we're discussing in the course of the book!).

🏃 Shift 29

OLD MINDSET: **Be likeable**
NEW MINDSET: **Be challenging**

When we were younger, we learned to contort ourselves so that our peers would like us. That was so important to us, to be liked and part of the gang. Feeling unliked was (and still is) hard to bear. This can lead to a 'People Pleaser' driver (Kahler 1975), where we do anything to please others, overriding our own needs and not setting boundaries as a result. As we saw in Shift 27, drivers are:

> [A] subconscious attempt by us to behave in ways that will gain us the recognition we need from others; they are also programmed responses to the messages we carry in our heads from important people in the past. (Hay 2009)

In coaching, the 'People Pleaser' driver can translate to being too nice. While there's nothing wrong with being pleasant and generous, this misses a vital element of coaching, which is to challenge. As mentioned previously, we may fear the backlash of challenge, but Blakey and Day (2012) asked leaders for feedback on their coaching and what would make it more impactful, and heard multiple times that these leaders wished to be challenged more.

Thinkers crave more challenge than we give them. Yet we under-challenge. We cosset. We protect. We collude.

Blakey and Day's Support and Challenge model shows us that we do need to have high support in place if we are to challenge in coaching. But support alone keeps us in the 'cosy corner', with our slippers on: it doesn't move the thinker anywhere near as far as when we add challenge into the mix. You may fear stressing them out (and not being liked), but that only happens if you aren't also demonstrating high support.

Challenge is not the same as conflict. Some coaches conflate the two. Challenge is positive (although conflict, when managed well, can be positive too). Challenge, when done compassionately, leads to breakthroughs. Challenge is not necessarily uncomfortable either, although it might make the thinker squirm a little to be asked the question they've been avoiding themselves, or to hear how they're being received by you.

Discomfort can be useful anyway. Enabling the thinker to stay in their comfort zone keeps them smaller than their potential. What's wrong with a little discomfort at the edge of their comfort zone if that shakes things up a bit? It's time to turn up the gas on the challenge we offer. They can take it. They won't dislike you as a result. Indeed, they will likely be grateful for it because it will take their thinking further.

I challenged a thinker about his stated commitment to his actions because I saw a look on his face that suggested that he wasn't, in fact, all that committed. As a result, we were able to get to the bottom of what was getting in his way. Had I ignored the facial expression and taken his commitment at face value, the obstacles may have prevented him from taking those actions. Despite initially feeling irked by the challenge, he was glad that we had surfaced the underlying barriers, so he could work around them to really commit to action.

Another example came in the middle of a session when a different thinker identified some shame associated with what she was saying. With permission, I took her into an exploration of the shame. Rather than allowing it to be a throwaway remark and colluding in glossing over it, we moved towards and into it to really get a handle on what it was, and how it was getting in her way. She may not have liked me much in that moment when I invited her into the shame, but she recognised how useful it was afterwards.

I let go of the need to be liked, knowing that challenge is more important.

That's not so very hard now, is it? I would posit that they will respect you more, not less, if you challenge those things that they know they need to be challenged on, but inadvertently avoid.

⏯ Shift 30

OLD MINDSET: Think about a clever response before they stop talking

NEW MINDSET: Don't think ahead; stay in the moment

Do you remember conversations with your peers where before they had even finished talking, you were thinking about a retort, getting your own viewpoint across or saying something witty?

It seems to be ingrained in us that we should think one step ahead of the other person. Why is that? What's the pay-off that led us to do it? Being liked, or seen as clever? Standing up for something?

Whatever it is, occasionally it creeps into coaching. Not so much getting your point of view across or some clever quip, but thinking ahead about your next question or observation. The thinker hasn't finished their thought process yet, so how do you know the question that you think of in this moment is going to be relevant when they do finish their thought? Even if it's just in two moments' time? Maybe there's a fear that you won't be ready with a perfectly formed question when they stop. Oh well!

Maybe you:

➡ don't like silence, so you don't want to leave your question formation until the pause – but silence is golden!

➡ have a sense of urgency and don't want to waste their time with a pause – it'll only be a second or two, and that pause allows new thinking to sink in for them

➡ hate looking as if you don't know what to say – it's back to that old chestnut of not needing to know (see also Shifts 27 and 40).

You'll need to decide for yourself what it is that's going through your mind as you concoct your question or observation too early.

What mindset should replace this? I tend to feel that the question or observation will present itself in the moment of pause, without my needing to prepare. I trust myself. I also trust the process. If a question or observation doesn't come to me in that moment, I use my trusty servant: the recontract.

➡ 'What are you aware of now that you were not aware of before – and where would be most useful to go next in our exploration?'

➡ 'Where are you in relation to your goal for today's coaching – and where do we need to go next to make more progress towards that?'

With these recontract questions, I'm also trusting the thinker: they can summarise where they've got to and where they want to go next. You don't need to do that for them. That means you don't need to hold all of the detail in your head while they are talking, either. You just need to be fully present.

Shift 31

OLD MINDSET: Here's what I would do
NEW MINDSET: What is going to work for you, given your personality and context?

When we are out for lunch with a friend or peer, it's easy to get caught up in giving advice based on our own experiences. It doesn't mean they will take that advice, but it's freely given. We're being helpful. But are we being useful? Whittington (2012) came up with the differentiation between helpful and useful:

➡ Helpful is doing something *for* someone. Useful is enabling them to do it *for themselves*.
➡ Helpful is rescuing. Useful is resourcing.
➡ Helpful is giving a man a fish; useful is teaching him to fish (Ritchie 1885).
➡ Helpful creates a dependency. Useful creates independence and self-sufficiency.

Being helpful isn't always that helpful, because the idea is something that worked for us, given our personality, context, values, stakeholders and situation, etc. Their personality, context, values, stakeholders, situation and so forth will be a different mix. A distinct set of ingredients, if you like, leading to a different cake!

I hear some coaches say that they can't see how they can possibly be adding value if they're not inserting ideas, options and choices for the thinker. What they're doing is infantilising the thinker, thinking that they, the parent, have a slew of answers to which the thinker doesn't have access. But the thinker has access to a completely different slew of answers, which better map to their way of seeing the world.

We don't add value by giving solutions. We add value by empowering thinkers to discover their own. We add value by enabling them to think, not just when we are with them, but when we are long gone. Our coaching equivalent of teaching them to fish is actually teaching them to think for themselves – and we don't teach them that by thinking for them. We teach them that by building that thinking muscle in them. We teach them that by asking questions rather than telling (see also Shifts 51 and 54). Enabling them to learn how to learn.

Even when thinkers ask you what you think, you can bat the question back such that they learn to think for themselves. They will sometimes ask for your thoughts in the session contract in answer to the question: 'How shall we work together today?' This is an opportunity for you to (re)lay down the boundaries of coaching.

Thinkers may ask you closer to the end of a session what you think. This is another opportunity for you to bat it back to them: 'What do *you* think about it?' They're so used to being spoon-fed (in conversation with peers or partners who give advice, or from parents, teachers or bosses), that it's no wonder they ask for your opinion. But it doesn't serve them in the long run, even though they might crave it in the moment.

Hold your ground. Ask them.

Ask, don't tell: 'What's going to work for you, given your personality and context?'

✻ Shift 32

OLD MINDSET: Breaking up is hard to do
NEW MINDSET: Ending is necessary

Did you ever have any friends who were no good for you or drained you? Or from whom you just drifted apart, but with a sense of guilt? It's worth looking at your pattern of endings. If you find them hard in life, you'll probably find them hard in coaching. We form attachments to people, so letting go can be hard.

The ultimate ending is death. What's your pattern when those close to you die? Do you say everything you want to say and make it a 'good', complete ending? Or do you leave things unsaid and realise too late that you can't now get closure?

If you're a parent, how hard was it to see your first child fly the nest? If you had a difficult experience with this ending, you'll likely have stored it in your body somehow, which will make future endings tricky too.

You may have had a dis-attachment from your carers earlier in life, which could make endings even more sensitive for you. What endings have been less than ideal for you? Perhaps too open-ended, not swift enough or out of your control?

Maybe you've had good experiences of endings in relationship with others.

All of these will have some bearing on how you end coaching conducts, whether they have come to term or finished earlier than anticipated.

Good, complete endings are necessary, so we need to get used to them. Without a good ending, we can't make a great new beginning (Bridges 2004). We're still attached in some way, which means we don't have the capacity for a great new beginning. We have baggage taking up space in our mind that we could do without to move forward.

There are two endings you need to think about in coaching:

1. The end of a session (see also Shifts 17 and 79).
2. The end of a programme of coaching.

Looking at the end of a programme of coaching, there are also two kinds:

1. Those that end as all the sessions are completed.
2. Those that come to an end earlier than expected.

Either way, it's important that you end well, with the thinker as your partner co-creating that ending, as this is their ending too.

You might ask questions by way of optional preparation for the last session, such as:

➡ 'Looking back on your original goals, what have you achieved as a result of coaching?'
➡ 'What else have you achieved as a result of coaching that you hadn't originally set out to achieve?'
➡ 'What limiting beliefs have you let go of?'
➡ 'What positive new beliefs do you have?'
➡ 'What specifically have you learned about yourself?'
➡ 'How is life different as a result of the learnings you've made during the coaching period?'
➡ 'What have you learned that you'll carry forward in life?'
➡ 'What are your top three goals and dreams in life right now (personal and work)?'
➡ 'What are your top five priorities in life, as you now understand them?'
➡ 'What support do you need to achieve those goals?'
➡ 'Who can provide that support?'
➡ 'How will you give yourself the space to reflect and strategise?'

It can be useful to get the thinker to pay attention to how they would like the coaching to end too with questions such as:

➡ 'What's your pattern of endings?'
➡ 'What beginnings are there for you in this ending?'
➡ 'How do you want this coaching to end?'

If a thinker goes AWOL (absent without leave) and doesn't come back for a final session, you'll need to think about how *you* mark the ending, how *you* celebrate what has been achieved, what new beginnings this makes possible for *you*. Otherwise, you may hold onto the unfinished business and not be able to move on.

Whatever happens, treat endings with the attention that they deserve. Mark the ending with a cake, card, gift, acknowledgement (see also Shifts 7 and 25) or something else of your choosing. Celebrate the work and the relationship. Prepare for the next chapter of their life.

Then, move on to pastures new.

 # Shift 33

OLD MINDSET: **Let's do this...**
NEW MINDSET: **How would it be if we did this...?**

As friends we might suggest doing things together, starting with: 'Let's...' Let's eat. Let's go to the cinema. Let's invite mum. It's a perfectly normal way of suggesting action of some kind – but it's directive, which means it doesn't belong in coaching. The coach who says 'let's' is influencing the thinker towards some action. For example: 'Let's pause for a moment and breathe.'

At face value, that might sound perfectly invitational. But it's you, the coach, who's deciding that this is what you need to do together now. The chances are that the thinker will follow, but they're being led. They're no longer in control of the agenda or where that goes.

It's subtle, but the marginal gain would be to shift to something like:

➡ 'How would it be if we paused for a moment and took a breath?'
➡ 'May I invite you to pause for a moment and breathe?'
➡ 'What do you need right now to be able to...?'

They can say 'no' to the first two, and the last one gives them free rein to decide whether it's a breath they need, or something completely different.

Subtle, marginal, but oh so powerful: giving the thinker choice. Choice is freedom. Choice is independence. Choice is a muscle that sometimes needs to be built. And you can help them to build that muscle by asking rather than directing.

 # Shift 34

OLD MINDSET: Silence is awkward
NEW MINDSET: Silence is golden thinking time

With our peers we learn to fill the silence. Maybe that's so another person can't fill it (linked to Shift 35, on being the loudest). We learn that silence is negative. I don't honestly get that, but for some people, silence feels awkward and needs to be filled. You may feel compelled to jump in and take the awkwardness away.

Unlike some of the habits I'm encouraging you to change, this one – filling the silence – just doesn't seem to serve any positive purpose. Why would you fill the silence, just for the sake of it? If you don't have something useful to say, don't say it – because if you do, that stops the thinker from using that silence to think, to work up something new and possibly insightful. Taking the air out of the room means you take away their thinking space.

In coaching, silence is golden thinking time. We need to get comfortable with it to allow for thinking space. New thinking doesn't trip off the tongue like known thinking does. New thinking needs time and space to percolate, form and be brought to the fore.

In conjunction with a set of coaches I was mentor-coaching, I've noticed that there is live silence and dead silence: they are hugely different. Live silence is when the thinker is obviously thinking. They'll be looking up, down, away into the distance, anywhere but at you. Their pace of talking will have slowed down. It will be more halting, as they join dots, one at a time. They may be more hesitant with this new thinking, making sense of it as they go.

They need the silence.

Dead silence is equally obvious to spot. The thinker will be looking straight at you, willing you to ask another question or make another observation. Usually, this is not a silence to extend, because they've stopped thinking at this point and need or want a nudge towards some more thinking. That nudge might be as simple as a recontracting question: 'Where do we need to go next to get to new thinking?'

If you're not a lover of silence, live silence is something to practise. Don't take the wind out of their thinking by talking over the live silence. Allow the silence to extend; allow them to continue their slower pace and meaning-making.

⚲ Shift 35

OLD MINDSET: The loudest voices have the most influence
NEW MINDSET: Being there is useful in itself

Quite often in peer groups, it's those who say the most and loudest who have the most influence. They make themselves heard. This is how they see themselves adding value to the group. Those who are more introverted make waves in different ways that add value, but the culture of allowing the loudest to be heard overshadows this. As a result, people start to believe that adding value is all about saying something.

It's not. We add value as coaches simply by being there, holding the space for the thinker to think, creating the environment where *they* can speak up and hear themselves think. There's no need for the coach to speak if the thinker is getting to new thinking. This is not 'doing nothing'; it is consciously holding the space for the thinker to process. As we've seen previously, interrupting because we don't think we have added value yet isn't useful.

I'm not saying you shouldn't speak at all – to ask about an emotive word that the thinker just used, for example, or to notice and explore their repeated use of another word. But you should also ask yourself to WAIT – Why Am I Talking? (source unknown):

➡ Am I talking to show that I am adding value?
➡ Am I talking to show off and be clever?
➡ Is my talking taking time away from their thinking?
➡ Am I interrupting their train of new thoughts?

When you listen to your coaching recordings, I recommend adding up the amount of time that you're talking in comparison with the thinker. What is the percentage split? There isn't an exact science for this, but if you're talking more than, say, 30 per cent of the time, start to ask yourself the questions above.

➡ Allow for silence, pause and reflection.
➡ Allow them to complete their thought if it's new thinking.
➡ Allow them to do most of the talking.

There is a balance here for sure, as your role is to get them to new thinking, not go over old ground. Again, as we've seen, listening to their context, background or story is not necessarily useful to them as they know this already, and have probably recited it to others before you. We *do* need to encourage them to get to new thinking by interrupting if we hear known thinking (see also Shift 4), but we can rest assured that our being there is useful in its own right.

Erik De Haan and Charlotte Sills (2012) found that relationship is key to the outcomes of coaching. While just being there is not the only part of a strong relationship, it does form part of it. Thinkers often say that this is the first time in their life that they have felt so listened to. Listening actively is one way that we build trust and safety for a thinker to continue with their thinking.

There's a difference between listening passively and actively, though. The active part is about noticing and exploring the words they use, their emotions and non-verbal expressions. These are all messengers of some kind, and your role as coach is to enable the thinker to hear the messages that these messengers (use of words, emotions, non-verbal expressions) bring.

Coaching *is* more than simply being there, with this active listening piece added in. It's enquiring about patterns you're noticing in their words and body language; exploring the emotions that are showing up; asking about the meaning they're making as they say things out loud, and asking not for the sake of hearing your own voice, but for their self-discovery. And don't think of it as 'just' being there. Being there is a strength in and of itself.

♡ Shift 36

OLD MINDSET: Don't air your dirty laundry in public

NEW MINDSET: Ask about mental health

Don't you just love some of the metaphorical language that we use in everyday parlance to mean something else? I don't remember anyone ever saying this phrase about airing your dirty laundry out loud in the system I grew up in, and yet it must have been there – otherwise how would I have remembered it?

What does it mean to 'air your dirty laundry in public?' *Collins' Dictionary*'s definition is to 'disapprove of others discussing or arguing about unpleasant or private things in front of other people'. What kinds of things constitute 'unpleasant or private things'? I'm sure that could be anything you want it to be, but in this case, I'm going to focus on mental health.

Mental Health First Aid England (n.d.) writes that: 'Although things are improving, stigma still exists around mental ill-health. As a society, we don't tend to know how to take care of our mental health like we do our physical health.'

Historically, it was taboo to ask about someone's mental health – seen as unpleasant or private and not something for others to enquire about. Mental Health First Aid training is now available to coaches to enable us to get over the fear of saying or doing the wrong thing, having deep conversations that are useful without crossing a perceived therapeutic boundary, or worrying about what might come out that we cannot 'contain'.

There might be red flags that lead you to ask what's going on for the thinker that might be getting in the way of their thinking. For example, if their 'stress container' (a name coined by Mental Health First Aid England, n.d.) appears to be overflowing with too many things that are causing them stress and anxiety, they appear to be exhausted as a pattern, or they're not taking any breaks in between meetings and not rehydrating, refuelling or re-oxygenating.

These are just some examples – you may have noticed many more in the course of your work. Even if they don't bring these as the focus for the coaching, they may drop them into the conversation as a passing comment. It's worth stopping to explore them, with the thinker's permission, as it's likely that these will get in the way of anything they are trying to work on in the coaching.

There is nothing 'dirty' about this particular laundry! It's a facet of modern life that we can help each other to work through if we're willing to ask the question: 'How are you *really*?' Also, to lean in when you notice a tremble in their voice, a tear in the corner of their eye, or if you notice yourself getting angry – as this might actually be their anger, not your own.

In mentor-coaching conversations, I often hear coaches say: 'But I'm not trained in therapy, so I choose not to ask about emotion, just in case it goes somewhere that I can't handle.' What I notice about this is that the coach and thinker miss so much richness of understanding about what the real issue is. If we don't lean in to explore the emotions together, we won't be able to work with what really needs to be addressed.

We can step back from that therapeutic cliff at any time, but often the coach is 20 paces away from the cliff, not even close – there's very little chance that you'll accidentally fall off it. Trust yourself that you'll know when you need to triage the situation rather than going closer to that edge. By triage, I mean stopping to discuss with the thinker whether coaching is still the most appropriate intervention, or whether in fact something else might be a better fit right now, or in tandem with the coaching.

Trust yourself that you – and they – can lean in to discussing present emotion, the meaning of it, the message it has for the thinker. And trust yourself that you'll know when you're no longer equipped to work with it and it needs a more experienced coach, therapist, doctor or someone else.

Trust the thinker too that they'll tell you if they don't want to discuss something – but ask whether they have somewhere else to take it.

⊛ Shift 37

With thanks to Yvette Elcock (Wiltshire-born, Black British, childless female, comprehensive education and college diploma, 61-year-old business owner, coach and coach supervisor) for co-writing this Shift.

> **OLD MINDSET: We avoid discussions of difference**
>
> **NEW MINDSET: We acknowledge our own and others' unique privilege and restriction**

How many times did someone in your family or peer group say: 'We just don't talk about that,' or 'shush' you when you started down that path? It might have been about money, politics, religion, beliefs, race, identity or mental health.

This mindset has certainly shifted in the past few years, as more people have spoken up about race and gender inequality or neuro-diversity. But how do we bring those kinds of conversations into coaching? Especially when there are so many white, middle-class, neurotypical female coaches in our industry who don't have the lived experience that some thinkers might have encountered? It's not that we need to have experienced the same events and suffering to be able to ask questions that help thinkers to think for themselves. But paying attention to context is important, as the ICF recognises in its competencies, where the coach:

➡ 'is sensitive to clients' identity, environment, experiences, values and beliefs' (ICF Competency 1: Demonstrates Ethical Practice)
➡ 'remains aware of and open to the influence of context and culture on self and others' (ICF Competency 2: Embodies a Coaching Mindset)
➡ 'seeks to understand the client within their context, which may include their identity, environment, experiences, values and beliefs' (ICF Competency 4: Cultivates Trust and Safety)
➡ 'demonstrates respect for the client's identity, perceptions, style and language and adapts one's coaching to the client' (ICF Competency 4: Cultivates Trust and Safety)

➡ 'considers the client's context, identity, environment, experiences, values and beliefs to enhance understanding of what the client is communicating' (ICF Competency 6: Listens Actively).

There's a pressing need for coaches to explore our own stance in a far more intersectional way, 'intersectional' meaning how our unique matrix of race, gender, neurodiversity, disability, age, caste, class, height, sexuality, belief or non-belief, etc. blends to make us who we are, and thinkers who they are. According to Kimberlé Williams Crenshaw (1989), this intersectionality shows our advantages and disadvantages, and will lead to empowerment or oppression.

The challenge is that any one element can create dis-comfort and dis-ease, let alone when multiple elements intersect and our unconscious bias gets in the way of us seeing thinkers as 'creative, resourceful and whole' (Whitworth et al. 1998). There is much work for us to do as coaches to understand our own unconscious bias. I recognised this in myself after a conversation with Katie Friedman (a neurodiverse coach specialising in coaching neurodiverse people) about neurodiversity, in which my bias showed up in my use of the phrase 'red flags'. I was alluding to some communication differences displayed by one of the thinkers with whom I'd worked. She challenged me to see the gold instead, the strengths rather than the deficits.

In a coaching session, you could ask:

➡ 'What areas might I need to pay more attention to more sensitively, in our work together?'
➡ 'What do I need to be aware of, here and now, as a [insert your intersectionalities] about this topic/issue that I don't know, and you do from your unique perspective?'
➡ 'What are the ethics that apply in this situation that might not be in my field of experience?'
➡ 'What "blind spots" might I have that are in full beam for you, as someone who is different to me?'
➡ 'I'm not an expert in motivating you, so may I encourage you to teach me how you learn, and how I might support and challenge you so that this coaching has high worth for you?'

You might notice that some of those questions are filling the coach in, and ordinarily I'd say that a coach should never ask questions to aid their own understanding. But these questions are still for the benefit of the thinker, as the answers enable the coach to ask questions in the coaching that are consciously *un*biased. They're part of our contracting, whether that is upfront or in the midst of the coaching.

Questions that might raise awareness for you both might include:

➡ 'What more do you want to say about how your environment is playing a part here?'
➡ 'How safe do you feel when working in this area or way?'
➡ 'I noticed a reaction in your eyes then; how has what I just said landed with you?'
➡ 'When I said X, what might have been a more meaningful word for you?'
➡ 'So, from your perspective, what else is going on here?'

As you self-supervise, you may want to ask yourself questions such as:

➡ In what ways are you and this thinker different?
➡ What might be at play here for you that's different from that for this thinker?
➡ If you look at the work of this session from a different context, what would that be, and how might it move you?

In all of these questions, we're shining a light on difference and ways that we and thinkers can rewrite our scripts.

Retrieval practice 3

It's time for some retrieval practice.

I know you're going to want to skip straight over this reflection piece, but by stopping for just a few minutes and writing down what your brain can retrieve, what you've read is more likely to stick and to be more easily accessed when you need it.

Here are some questions for you to write the answers to:

➡ What do you recall from this chapter?
➡ What rings true to you?
➡ What do you see more clearly now?
➡ How does this feel in your body?
➡ What else do you sense?
➡ Which mindsets do you want to discard to make way for more transformational mindsets?
➡ What else did your peers instil in you that you could discard to be a more masterful coach?

Habit change commitment 3

It's time to commit to trying something different, based on what has resonated with you. This template will help you to make *one* commitment to make *one* small change. When you're comfortable with that, you can make another, and another.

➡ Instead of believing the voice in my head that says...
➡ Which leads me to do/say...
➡ I choose to believe...
➡ And will therefore do/say...
➡ My cue or reminder is...
➡ My immediate reward will be...

You may choose to share this commitment with a coaching buddy for more social accountability.

Now, stop reading and writing: go and experiment with what you have learned, before coming back for more mindset shifts in the rest of the book.

Chapter 4

Mindsets we learned from work that we need to discard to be a more masterful coach

The working world has certain expectations of how we behave. Not every workplace will be the same, but I suspect you'll relate to many of these. The coaches I interviewed certainly recognised many of these expectations and mindsets. Those expectations will have shaped the person we are today and how we show up as coaches.

The story of my working life started as a Saturday job in a bakery, surrounded by bread and cakes! Here, I learned to be customer focused. During my time at university, I worked in a stationery shop, surrounded by writing accoutrements. I learned more customer focus. During my holidays, I worked in a pub and a hotel in Jamaica – more customer focus.

After university, I worked in a department store while I was saving to go on a round-the-world trip – more customer focus. Are you detecting a theme here? When I came back from travelling, I started on a graduate programme in a bank. Credit risk and researcher (a breakaway from customer service), PA to a director (back to customer service), and then into learning and development.

That's where I've remained ever since, in some shape or form, enabling others to learn how to learn. This is where coaching came into my life 20-plus years ago, as it's all about learning to learn, learning to think for oneself about oneself.

My very last role in corporate life was in human-centred design, where I interviewed employees to discover their exact needs and desires, so that these could be fed into the design of new processes and systems that would meet those needs and desires. I found that employees left those interviews feeling clearer about what they wanted from a career, and often had actions to take and conversations in mind that would take them closer to their own needs and desires. A bit like coaching!

I share all of this with you to give you a taste of the kinds of mindsets that I might have developed while I worked for small and large organisations. Your working history might be different, but I'm betting you'll recognise many of the mindsets I describe in this chapter.

As you think about what work taught you, explicitly or implicitly, what have you already discarded to be a more masterful coach? What might you need to continue to discard to become an even better coach for the thinkers with whom you will work in future?

Stop for a moment and reflect on that, before reading on to see what I've noticed alongside the people I've interviewed.

🛠️ Shift 38

OLD MINDSET: Act like a service provider
NEW MINDSET: Be a partner, so thinkers can move out of consuming and into thinking for themselves

At work, many of us have learned to be a service provider, whether to meet the needs of external customers or internal stakeholders. You may still be in that organisational world and experiencing it, or it may be in your past. Either way, you are likely to have experience in the working world around being a service provider.

We also expect(ed) others around us to act like service providers. What does that service mentality look or sound like?

➡ 'How can I help you?'
➡ 'What do you need from me?'
➡ 'I'll get that to you as soon as possible.'
➡ 'Value = a solution.'
➡ 'I'll go over and above to provide you with value.'
➡ 'Don't come to me with problems; come to me with solutions.'

I could go on, but I'll let you think about all the occasions when you've provided a service at work. In that context, that might have been exactly what was needed (although I contend that we jump too high much of the time when setting boundaries might be more useful).

In coaching, we need to shake off this service provider mentality because it creates a power dynamic that's not useful. Every time you do something for the thinker that they could do for themselves, they embrace the consumer mindset. The more they become a consumer, the less thinking they will do for themselves, so you create a vicious cycle.

The problem starts well before you start coaching. You sell coaching, one person or organisation buying from another. That sets it up as a service in a way that doesn't attend to the thinker's real needs. Unfortunately, when they see it as a service, they expect (perhaps subconsciously) to be served. Not only that, but at school and in other learning situations, thinkers have been used to being students. Subconsciously again, they might see this coaching as an extension of a student–teacher relationship. It's not!

As we've identified previously, the most valuable service you can provide is to encourage them to think – to build and sustain their own thinking muscles. But that feels like hard work to the thinker. It's not what they expect of a service provider who'd normally make things easier for them, not harder: so that selling piece gets in the way of the partnership that you need to create – a partnership where your role as coach is to help the thinker to think rather than thinking for them, and their role is to think and then be different and act differently. Their role and responsibilities in this partnership require a lot from them.

Right from the start of the coaching (and even before that, as part of our sales), you, the coach, need to speak of this as a partnership, and act accordingly. Coach and thinker are travelling into the unknown together, not to some pre-determined product or outcome.

First things first: let's move away from calling the people we work with a 'client' – which assumes some kind of service. Let's also not call them 'the coachee', as this assumes that they'll be having coaching done to them (Benjamin 2017) rather than being in partnership. A partnership is different from a service provider–consumer relationship. It's a meeting of equals.

Once you start the work with the thinker, the two of you co-create the coaching agreement, both the 'Big C Contract' and the session contract (see also Shifts 2 and 3) as a way of partnering. You need to be transparent about the time you have to play with; and you continue to be transparent about that, so that in partnership, the two of you can manage the time you have together to be most useful for the thinker.

You need to:

➡ ask them where they want to start, rather than deciding for them
➡ continue to ask them where they want to take their thinking next, rather than presuming that you know the best direction to take it
➡ talk about 'we' – e.g. 'How shall *we* do this work *together* today?' rather than 'What would you like from me today?'
➡ let the thinker know that they can push back at any time if something is not working for them, or if there is a different question or direction that they need to pursue

➡ be OK with not knowing, and walk alongside the thinker as they start to discover their own knowing (see also Shifts 27 and 40).

Resist invitations from the thinker to move into the mentoring, teaching or consultancy that they almost inevitably will request, because that's the student or consumer habit – and it's hard to break.

When I asked a thinker with whom I've been partnering for some time how he'd like us to work together that day, he half-jokingly said: 'Can you just tell me what I should do?'

We laughed and I replied: 'You know that's not going to happen,' and we moved back into him doing the thinking for himself. He did know that I wasn't going to give him advice – but sometimes when you're working with someone new, they won't know that this isn't how coaching works.

You can gently remind the thinker that coaching draws on their inner wisdom, and that only they know deep down what would work for them. For example, telling someone to paint as a way to release tension isn't going to work for other people in the same way as it does for me, so there's no point in my offering that up as a solution when they can find their own, better fitting ones.

Stay in 'Adult' mode, rather than 'Parent'; inviting them to be in 'Adult' mode with you (Berne 1964) to stretch and build their own thinking muscle. Even when you're pinning them down to action, stay in 'Adult' mode. This isn't about the teacher setting homework that the student must do or fail.

The same goes for checking in on the thinker's progress – this shouldn't feel as if they're reporting back to their teacher. You don't want to induce shame if they haven't done what they said they were going to do – they may well have chosen to do something else instead that still moved them forwards or was a higher priority. Rather than asking: 'What have you achieved since last time?', ask them: 'What are you learning about yourself in between sessions?'

Don't presume that all of the learning and thinking happens in the coaching sessions – if you partner in wrapping up the session in a way that enables them to commit to next steps, the thinker will continue to think and grow on their own.

What else do you notice about creating a partnership in coaching?

☞ Shift 39

OLD MINDSET: Be the fixer
NEW MINDSET: Be the resourcer

I notice that some coaches hold on to the belief that the value they bring to thinkers is in the ideas they give to those thinkers, the solutions they offer, the benefit of their experience. It's no wonder when that's what coaches were (or still are) paid for as employees of an organisation: to fix things that are broken, design and create things that need to be made or make continuous improvements to their work and workplace. To come up with solutions and ideas, drawing on the benefit of their experience.

At work, you may have developed a 'go above and beyond' mindset of being helpful to others and showing that you're thinking about your internal or external clients and their needs. This will get you Brownie points, if not a pay rise or bonus for being at the upper end of the performance curve, doing more than your peers. That performance curve, where people are rated according to the value they add, drives behaviours around doing more – especially that others will notice.

According to Koroleva (2016), in coaching this solution orientation provides a short-term fix and doesn't necessarily lead to long-term sustainable change. But it's ingrained in us, as we've had it instilled in us over so many years. Your employed job is (or was) to fix problems, have answers, tell others what to do. Let's look at how this might harm others with whom you are working in a coaching scenario.

In Transactional Analysis terms, this is known as being 'the Rescuer', a term coined by Karpman (1968) as one corner of the Drama Triangle. The Rescuer:

➡ discounts the autonomy of the thinker and their power to help themselves
➡ believes their own needs are not important and discounts these as well, draining their own energy levels
➡ takes responsibility for doing things that the thinker should or could do themselves.

Coaches don't always know they are doing this, or if they do, they defend their actions by saying this is how they add value. But they deplete long-term value, as they aren't building the thinker's thinking muscle.

In coaching you need to do less, not more. You need to step away from the 'What can I do to help?' mentality. I don't mean that we need to be *un*helpful, but that we can be too helpful at times. Being helpful can infantilise others. It can cause them to be reliant on us and others. It might even cause the thinker to be inadvertently lazy: for example, if you were to look something up on the Internet for them after a session when they're quite capable of doing that for themselves.

I feel as though there is a crossover here with the way we behave in the business development cycle. Being generous with what we share with others can get us new business. But how much should we share once we are in the Adult-to-Adult relationship of coaching, as Berne (1964) describes it?

If we look at the more useful way of being, we find 'the Resourcer', one corner of Choy's (1990) Winner's Triangle, sometimes also known as 'the Carer'. The Resourcer still cares for the other, but shows their care in a different way. They:

➡ listen to the thinker without solving their problems for them
➡ respect and draw on the thinker's abilities to think, feel and ask for their needs to be met, recognising their autonomy to help themselves
➡ take responsibility for their own feelings and needs, and have good boundaries around those
➡ treat the thinker as an Adult rather than a Child (Berne 1964).

I'm sure you learned about the Drama and Winner's Triangles in your coach training – but it's one thing understanding the model at an intellectual level, and quite another to put it into practice when those old script patterns from work keep tempting you back to add value by giving advice.

Hawkins and Smith (2013) wrote: 'The work of the learning enabler is never to know better, and never to know first but to create the enabling conditions.' Maybe we do have some helpful information to share – but by sharing it, are we knowing best, or proving that we know more?

We need to shake off these more directive *helpful* (see also Shift 31) ways of being, and embrace being *useful* by resourcing others to help themselves. Unless, that is, there really is only one answer: for example:

➡ a policy that states the action the thinker must take in this context
➡ a health and safety directive that makes it clear what needs to happen in a certain instance
➡ a law that must be followed
➡ if there's a fire and you all need to evacuate.

What is going to work for you to break this mindset and habit of fixing and move towards resourcing?

⬡ Shift 40

OLD MINDSET: Be an expert in your field
NEW MINDSET: Enter a coaching session without memory, desire or understanding

Unless we were a generalist, the culture at work may have encouraged us to become an expert in something, to get deep knowledge and understanding of our field. Being seen as the 'go-to' person is a badge of honour. That's totally reasonable, as knowledge workers are paid for their expertise.

Coaches need to develop an expertise in coaching and this book aims to support you in that, making marginal gains that sharpen your coaching edge. But we don't need to be an expert in the *thinker's* field. From a marketing viewpoint, it can help if the buyer believes us to have been there and done that, but we can still coach without this.

As we saw in Shift 17, we don't need to understand everything that the thinker says.

There is a problem here, though: the expectations of the thinker we're coaching and the budget-holder (often human resources, learning and development or the thinker's manager, if the organisation for whom the thinker works is the buyer). They may expect us to be an expert, or more of a mentor or teacher – so part of our contracting and continued recontracting will require us to be clear about this.

It's more important that we approach each session without perceived understanding because believing we know can have two impacts: first, we might lead them to an answer that may or may not be useful to them; second, we collude with them in the same set of assumptions they are making, rather than testing those.

Wilfred Bion (1967) said that the practitioner should 'impose on himself a positive discipline of eschewing memory and desire. I do not mean that "forgetting" is enough: what is required is a positive act of refraining from memory and desire'.

Come into each session without any preconceived notions, and no memory of what happened last time because, as we've already identified, the thinker will have moved on since then (see Shift 21 about note-taking in relation to memory). Come with no desire to fix or supply a solution, or have anything happen other than what unfolds and emerges in the session right there between the two of you in partnership.

How would that be for you to turn up without memory or desire? What would be different to the way you currently approach your sessions?

For me, that's about not taking responsibility for keeping the thinker on track in any way. They're an adult, and my role is to help them to keep themselves on track.

It's about approaching each session with the thinker in my mind's eye as they come into the session, not as they were at the end of the last one.

It's about having a metaphorical and literal blank sheet of paper (that hardly gets any notes added to it in the course of the session, at my end at least).

It's about not knowing.

Not knowing is the antithesis of being an expert.

🐌 Shift 41

OLD MINDSET: Work as quickly as you can
NEW MINDSET: Get to what matters most, then slow down to explore

These days, work requires us to move at pace, to get as much done as we possibly can in the time we have (and to extend the time we have to get even more done – a false presumption of course, as we get increasingly less productive in those extra hours we spend working). Greater productivity is the zenith: getting more done with less.

The 'Hurry Up' driver, first named by Kahler (1975), plays a part here (see also Shift 27 for an explanation of drivers). As the name suggests, the people with this driver rush around, getting as much done as they can without stopping to smell the roses. They may eat, walk and talk fast.

The Hurry Up-driven person is often lauded at work for getting a lot done. And it's understandable that workplace cultures encourage this Hurry Up driver, as they want higher levels of productivity. But in coaching we're more about getting to what matters most as soon as we can, then exploring the territory. And again, as we've noted previously, that exploration of the territory doesn't necessarily need 90 minutes or 2 hours: we can make huge shifts in 30 minutes of coaching – *if* we establish what matters most at the start of a session.

The aim of coaching is not to be productive, but to evoke awareness. Evoking awareness may lead to ideas, options and solutions, but understanding the underlying issue, root cause or belief is the progress that's most needed first. This is why we need to slow down once we know what it is we're working on.

I was working with someone who wanted to work out his future next steps with regard to business development. We could have launched straight into tasks, but we realised together that it was his underlying beliefs and values that needed to drive his next steps, not the instructions of a marketing expert to do X, Y and Z that were incongruent with who he is.

We're back to CONTRACTing (see also Shift 3) as our way of getting to what matters most. As Michael Bungay Stanier (2016) pointed out, good coaches meander and take time to get to what matters most. Great coaches get there sooner, so that the rest of the time can be used to move forward with what matters most.

CONTRACTing doesn't mean that we rush through all of the questions before the coaching begins. The CONTRACT *is* the coaching, and the thinker will be making progress while getting real clarity on their question. Imagine the CONTRACT phase like the ebb and flow of the sea or an accordion, sucking in air and blowing it out (see also Shift 14). Coach and thinker will still pause to reflect on non-CONTRACT questions that unpack what's being said or not said, and your focus is on channelling to what matters most for the session.

The question may still change as the session unfolds, in which case you recontract, but at least you had a question to get started.

Hawkins and Smith (2013) developed the CLEAR model:

Contract
Listen
Explore
Action
Review.

You'll notice that Listen and Explore come before Action. I often see coaches moving beyond Exploration and into Action quickly with questions such as: 'What do you think you'll do about that?' The problem with this is that the actions are then transactional: there hasn't been enough exploration of the beliefs and mindset preventing the thinker from changing. If we don't get underneath the surface to these beliefs and values, any actions that the thinker decides on will slip back in due course, as they fall back on those old beliefs.

To get underneath the surface, we might ask questions such as:

➡ 'What are you believing about yourself that is stopping you from making a change?'
➡ 'What assumptions are implicit in what you just said?'
➡ 'What is important to you about that?'

– or any other question that goes vertically: deeper, under the surface (see also Shifts 46 and 63).

Going deeper in this way enables the two of you to go slow at this exploration phase, so as to be able to go fast to the actions that fall out of the beliefs and mindsets at the back end of the coaching session. Don't be afraid to slow down and go deeper in this way after the CONTRACT, as this leads to actions that are more transformational, aligned and authentic for the thinker.

What we're learning here is that getting to action is not what matters most – getting to transformation is. Getting underneath the surface, exploring the territory such that the route to resolution is grounded in what matters most: beliefs and values.

Shift 42

OLD MINDSET: Always be serious
NEW MINDSET: Be playful and experimental

Did you learn to be serious at work? I did. Sure, I had a laugh with my colleagues every now and again, but generally we were all about getting our heads down and doing the serious work of work, that was the culture. More recently, when I was in a human-centred design team, we played a lot more!

As a coach, I've been experimenting with more playful ways of being. Ways that tap into multiple intelligences, not just the logical brain. Calling forth both my creative child and that of the thinkers with whom I'm partnering.

Maybe that's the problem: we think of play and creativity as childish. If we were to think of it as child*like*, drawing on that other part of us that has so much to offer, perhaps we would be more playful, be more experimental, dance, sing, write poetry, move.

Steve Ridgley (coach, coach supervisor and formerly Manager of Learning and Growth at the John Lewis Partnership) and I recorded a podcast with Rowan Gray about movement (Norman and Ridgley 2021), and noted just how restricted workplaces are culturally around movement. We sit at our desks at work, side-by-side or webcam-to-webcam as coach and thinker. And yet using their body can and does bring thinkers new insights that the brain can't access (see also Shift 62).

Standing can help a thinker to see things from a new perspective. So can moving to different parts of the room that represent different viewpoints, and accessing those viewpoints as though the thinker were that person; moving to a place in the room that represents the future, really inhabiting it and using what they sense there to inform the present; and walking (together side-by-side or apart by phone). The list of possibilities goes on.

Drawing, even if it's just one mark on the paper that's representative of a relationship, can give a thinker so much new awareness that they wouldn't get from talking *about* the relationship (or another topic on which they are hoping to get more clarity).

Invite the thinker to use objects around them to represent parts of themselves, their system or a problem to bring new knowing that they wouldn't necessarily get from auditory processing. Each object shows them something in a new light.

I did this recently with a thinker, asking him to choose objects that might give him a new perspective about the brand that he wanted to portray. He chose items at random from around the room and as he looked at each one, they gave him some new wisdom that he wouldn't have accessed simply by thinking more.

Or invite the thinker to place objects (buttons, plectrums or any objects that the thinker has on the desk) in relation to one another out in front of them, to help map out a picture of connection (or lack of connection) as they notice distance, direction, size, etc. And we, the coach, don't need to be able to see any of these, so we can use them over virtual media just as well as we could use them face-to-face.

Nature can show up things we wouldn't otherwise notice too, whether that's using items from nature or its metaphors. For example, in a walking coaching session with a thinker, we stopped for a moment to look at the shimmer of the sun gleaming off the river, and I asked what wisdom that offered her in relation to her conundrum. We can also draw on more general metaphors.

The thing is, you need to create the best experiments in the moment, unplanned and unprepared. Something that comes to mind in the moment will land far better, writes John Leary-Joyce (2014), than some pre-prescribed exercise that doesn't quite fit for the thinker.

What else can you do to bring play and creativity into the coaching 'room' (I use this term loosely, as we may not even be in a room, virtual or otherwise; we may be getting creative by walking, cycling together or even lying on our backs, looking up at the sky). Any of these will evoke different awareness in the thinker, compared with what they would access simply by talking.

Bear in mind, though, that you should *invite* them into these experiments rather than directing them there. Something like:

➡ 'I wonder whether you might find it useful to draw what is going on, so that you can access new thinking. What do you think?'

➡ 'I have an experiment in mind. May I explain it briefly and you can say whether you think it will be useful to you?'

If they decline, that's their prerogative. Enforced creativity this is not! Neither is it play for its own sake. It's all for the purposes of new thinking.

1 Shift 43

OLD MINDSET: Be more efficient by multitasking

NEW MINDSET: Be more effective by single-tasking

At work, there's always a lot to juggle. You may have developed a knack for multitasking: 'dealing with multiple task demands concurrently by improvising, rearranging, and interleaving planned tasks with unexpected tasks' (as defined by Loukopoulos et al. 2009).

That's the reality of the working world today, which is rarely linear and much more likely to consist of multiple 'swim-lanes'. You may be good at it. It may have served you well in accomplishing all that you needed to get done. But in coaching, we cannot multitask. When we are with a thinker, we aim for a singular focus on them, bringing ourselves into total presence with them, so that we can pick up both on the nuances of what they say and how they say it, and anything that's happening in our own body which might be a reflection of what's going on for them.

When multitasking is in our bones, it can be hard to be so unequivocally attentive to this one person. It can take practice to turn away from distractions. When you think of the things that distract you from being fully present with a thinker, what might those be for you?

If you're working in a busy location with people moving around you or talking in proximity, this will break your attention, even for a split second – so choosing a location where neither of you will be distracted is important.

If you're working from home, the distractions of a busy household could get in your way. People have been much more accepting of barking dogs or lorry-reversing beeps, but these things still take attention away from the thinking environment for both parties – so you need to do what you can to avoid them.

Setting up both yourself *and* the thinker for good thinking is crucial. You may not have control over their environment, but you can remind them what makes for good thinking space.

If you're using technology such as Zoom or Microsoft Teams, computer pings can get in the way of single-tasking: please turn off any instant messages or pop-ups so as not to divert your attention. I also invite you to turn off your self-view, so you aren't distracted by seeing yourself in the mirror, so to speak. Put your phone onto airplane mode (or better still, leave it outside the room, as research tells us that even having it switched off face down in the room causes a distraction, Ward et al. 2017).

To focus fully, let go of all of the external pressures that you face, both personal and professional. You can't work right up until the time you get onto a coaching call because you'll still be holding the vestiges of that work as you enter the coaching 'room'. In particular, the mindsets that guided you in that work may not be those you need for coaching. Having a buffer in between that other work and this coaching will give you the opportunity to switch mindsets in a conscious way. Just as importantly, encourage thinkers not to book meetings back-to-back with their coaching. Both coach and thinker need space to get ready for, and decompress from, the coaching (see also Shift 13).

Getting ready for the coaching also includes letting go of what's on your mind and to-do list. How you use that slot before a coaching session to get ready is up to you – you'll know what allows you to be fully present, whether that's holding the thinker in mind and believing them to be creative, resourceful and whole, meditating, taking a walk or something else that works for you.

What else do you need to put in place to enable you to single-task and focus on the thinker during your time together?

🏋 Shift 44

OLD MINDSET: Consultancy perpetuates dependency

NEW MINDSET: Coaching leads to independent, critical thinkers and decision makers

If you've ever worked in a consultancy, you may recognise the underlying raison d'être to *increase* the scope of work, as you discover more of what needs fixing. The client needs the consultant to fix the glitches. The more the consultant does, the more the client relies on them. The more the consultant does, the more issues they find that need fixing, and the cycle continues. This may be a slight exaggeration – not all consultants have that mindset – but there is an element of truth to the upsell.

Coaching is about doing yourself out of a job. Your aim is to enable the thinker to:

➡ learn how to think for themselves
➡ draw on their own inner resourcefulness to resolve their dilemmas, issues and opportunities
➡ recognise their own resourcefulness in the first place
➡ become confident in themselves
➡ increase their self-esteem.

The aim is for them to become bigger, bolder and more able to deal with life and work conundrums. You need to want to become redundant. Or at least you should.

Money gets in the way, though. It's easier to keep a current client than to find and sign up a new one, so you may be tempted to continue working with a thinker after their programme of coaching is complete. But is that really what's right for them? Are you becoming a crutch for them?

There will always be more work to be done with a thinker. We're all a work-in-progress. Learning and growing go on for our whole life, but a thinker could do that learning and growing alone for a while. It's dangerous to believe that they need us in perpetuity. They don't. If you do your job well, thinkers will develop into *independent*, critical thinkers and decision makers.

What questions are you asking yourself and the thinker when they come to the end of a contract and ask to continue?

Do you raise an internal cheer about the extra money it will bring in?

Do you feel drawn to completing what you both started, when they may be able to keep the momentum going alone?

How do you assess whether it's time for them to cut the apron strings?

How will you enable the thinker to be independent of you, after the coaching programme has ended?

🏛 Shift 45

OLD MINDSET: I am responsible for the outcome

NEW MINDSET: I am responsible for the coaching process, the thinker is responsible for the outcome and their future

At work, you are responsible for the outcome of your work. You have goals and objectives, and are expected to make those a reality, with or without others. This is what you're measured against: whether and how you hit your targets. But in coaching, the coach is responsible for the coaching *process*, not the *results*:

➡ creating trust and safety so that the thinker can be vulnerable

➡ being wholly present and holding the space for great thinking

➡ contracting for the session outcomes, measures of success and ways of working together

➡ listening actively to enable you to enquire about and explore their words, emotions and non-verbal cues

➡ asking questions and noticing to evoke awareness

➡ closing the session in such a way that the thinker continues to experiment and grow post-session.

While you hold responsibility for the process, the thinker has responsibility for their own outcomes and future. As we've seen previously, this is a hard habit to break for some coaches, who hold too tightly onto the idea that they must get the thinker to a resolution or action right there in the session. Yes, you want them to have made progress, but any progress is good progress (Amabile and Kramer 2011), even without a fully formed action plan.

➡ Action plans, solutions and tying up all the loose ends are *corporate* requirements.

➡ Progress, new thinking and new awareness are *coaching* requirements.

Let go of the outcome of the session. The thinker will get to wherever they get to and if there's a gap between what they said they wanted and where they've got to, that's OK. They can continue thinking about this after the coaching is over if they choose to – that is their decision and responsibility. You're simply the conduit for their thinking, the creator of a great thinking environment. You're not responsible for driving to answers. In fact, driving the session leads to transactional results rather than transformation, as you'll likely have worked at a superficial level. The thinker is an adult, and they're perfectly capable of taking responsibility for discovering (through your managing the process and alone) and working towards their own outcomes. They may or may not do what they say they are going to do. That's their call, not yours.

You may need to manage the expectations of both the thinker and their sponsor upfront: that the thinker is responsible for the outcome, it's up to them to make any changes they want to make, there is no magic wand, and understanding themselves better will enable them to make more transformational change than they would if you were to focus purely on quick marching towards a trans-actional outcome.

Let go of the outcome of the session or programme. By letting go, I promise you that more will happen than you thought possible.

⍟ Shift 46

OLD MINDSET: Don't ask a question unless you know the answer

NEW MINDSET: Ask questions that lead to new knowing

In a courtroom, a defendant's lawyer will only ask questions to which they know the answers: they don't want to be surprised or hear new thinking. Their preparation ahead of the trial means that they know exactly what questions they'll ask, and exactly what answers will be given.

Coaches are not working in a courtroom. Your job is not to ask questions that get to known thinking, but to ask questions that lead to new knowing.

I hear coaches asking questions that fill them in on information, such as:

➡ 'What is your supervisor's name?'
➡ 'Do you drive?'
➡ 'What are the facilities available at that gym?'

The thinker already knows the answers to these information-gathering and solution-offering questions. They don't need to waste time going over this old ground. It's as though the coach is gathering information in order to make a diagnosis and offer a cure, as a doctor might do. Or the coach is like a salesperson, who gathers information to match their product to those needs. Joining the dots when the thinker can do that for themselves when they become aware of what those dots are.

Questions that lead to new knowing are more likely to go vertical rather than forwards horizontally. For example:

➡ 'What is the meaning of [word that they used]?'
➡ 'What's the significance of [emotion they described]?'
➡ 'Where do you feel that in your body?'
➡ 'What does your beating heart have to tell you?' (After they

mentioned that their heart is beating fast.)

These types of questions keep the thinker focused on the present and what's becoming apparent to them right here in this moment. They don't go backwards over old ground, or forwards to a solution. They stick with the here and now to evoke new awareness. They're curious, not nosy (see also Shifts 17, 24 and 68). They're client-centred rather than coach-centred.

They're of their moment. They'll never be used again, as they're only relevant at that time. And they are all about new thinking.

If you have the mindset of a lawyer, doctor or salesperson, it's time to shift to that of a coach, whose job is to evoke new thinking by going vertically beneath the surface, not horizontally forwards. Forward momentum comes more swiftly later in the arc of the coaching, once the thinker understands themselves through new knowing.

🏃 Shift 47

OLD MINDSET: Don't bring your home life into work

NEW MINDSET: Enable the thinker to bring their whole self to coaching

This idea of not bringing your home life to work may have shifted over the course of the Covid-19 pandemic, where we were all working from home and life was more transparent. It showed up behind us on our webcam, in the form of children wanting attention or pets climbing into the video frame. We brought each other into our homes, although we may have blurred out the background to keep some privacy.

Despite that shift, the belief that we should keep work and life separate seems to be prevalent in the way that some workers and managers get straight into talking about the task at hand when meeting virtually. They miss the serendipitous meetings at the coffee machine or in the lift, where they ask people how their weekend was, or lunching together to get to know each other as people.

Coaching is not about task-only. As identified previously, we coach the person, not the problem (Franklin 2019, Reynolds 2020; see also Shift 19). We need to let go of solutions and embrace evoking awareness. Ultimately, evoking awareness leads to a better solution, but we can't put the cart before the horse.

Neither is coaching just about the thinker's work life. Even if their company is paying, the thinker can bring anything they wish to coaching because it will have an impact on how they show up at work. We can't separate what's happening at home from work. If the thinker is going through a divorce (whether amicable or acrimonious), that's going to show up in some form at work. If they're working long hours, that's going to affect their home life. This applies to us as the coach too, of course, and you need to take care of your own needs in this respect (see also Shift 13).

I let people know at the start of a coaching contract that they can bring anything, but they don't always hear that at the beginning.

I've had someone ask whether it was OK to talk about his wife asking to split up from him because it was the most important thing in his life. You won't be surprised to learn that I said of course he could. His whole life would be different as a result, including his work. He needed a place to figure out what that new life might look like for him once he had processed the grief, sadness and despair.

We need to help thinkers (and their organisational sponsors) to let go of the idea that we can compartmentalise work and life, and leave life at the (metaphorical or physical) door. This belief is old-fashioned anyway, but even more out of kilter with the philosophy of coaching.

 # Shift 48

> **OLD MINDSET: Businesspeople are hard-nosed and harsh**
>
> **NEW MINDSET: Boundaries around time, fees and so forth are professional**

I was once accused of being 'too corporate' in the way I managed my working boundaries around roles and responsibilities. I understand that different organisations have differing cultures, but I don't accept that people should bend over backwards to compensate for others' lack of planning.

As a result of my corporate 'upbringing', I do set strong boundaries around time, fees, cancellations, no-shows, roles and responsibilities and do my best to stick to those because I see them as useful – and professional.

Let's take cancellations and no-shows, for example. When I was an internal coach, I was fine financially if someone cancelled a coaching session with me at the last minute because I was still getting paid whether they showed up or not.

But it still broke our agreement around the thinker committing to their learning and growth. It showed a lack of respect for me, the coach, as I'd planned my day and my work around the thinker. It also shows a lack of respect for the thinker themselves, as they put themselves and their needs at the bottom of the pile of things to address.

Certainly, there are times when a cancellation is necessary, such as when a family member or the thinker themselves is sick. Or when there's a safeguarding issue in the workplace, such as in a school or a charity that works with children. But in my mind, people place the wrong emphasis on urgency for other things, when (usually) no one is going to die if the thinker says they'll get back to it after their coaching. Thinkers sometimes don't plan their time well enough to be able to give themselves the gift of coaching time.

Now that I'm an external coach, I have the added reason for

being strict with cancellations, in that I can't replace paid work at a moment's notice, nor even at two or three days' notice. Sure, I always have other work that needs to be done, but it's not paid work and I need to make a living just like the next person.

I discuss this in my contracting with thinkers, so they know to give me a five-day notice of postponement, except in the above exceptional circumstances. If I'm collaborating with them under an organisational contract, I make sure the organisation and the line manager are clear on this too, so that they don't expect the thinker to drop their coaching in favour of work. Coaching is the work after all. It's not an optional extra.

I'm also clear on both my and their role – my role isn't to advise or teach or mentor. As outlined previously, the thinker's role is to do the hard thinking for themselves. And I stress the line manager's role too, so they don't get the impression that they can outsource their managerial responsibilities to me. I use the wording below, in an email, to help the manager to understand their role.

> Coaching is exponentially more successful if you, the manager, are an integral partner in the process and give support and feedback on progress on a day-to-day basis.
> I would ask you to:
>
> ➡ work with the thinker to identify strengths, development areas and issues to be addressed before coaching commences
> ➡ provide input on areas for goal-setting for the coaching
> ➡ clarify expectations
> ➡ make the needed resources available
> ➡ release them from their work to attend coaching sessions on time
> ➡ encourage and celebrate wins
> ➡ give feedback on progress on a regular basis
> ➡ respect the confidentiality of the coaching relationship: don't ask me for an update – ask the thinker instead, so they can decide what they wish to share with you.

When it comes to time boundaries, I agree with the thinker how long a session will be, then we stick to that. I start, stay and stop on time (or they forfeit the time if they are late), because I know that a thinker may have made other plans they need to attend to after our session. If I were to overrun, their amygdala may start firing as they get worried about being late, and as soon as that happens, they stop thinking well.

These are my boundaries and I make them transparent upfront as I see this as part of creating trust and safety. As we've seen, just like children, adults also need boundaries to function well. Boundaries show that we mean business. You can decide on your own boundaries, and you have choices about whether you flex them for certain reasons; without them, you may come across as disorganised, submissive and unprofessional.

Remember: this is a partnership, not a transactional service provision, and for that you both need to articulate your needs and have them met. You're setting a good example by voicing your needs, rather than falling into 'Victim' mode on Karpman's Drama Triangle (1968), by complaining behind their back.

Retrieval practice 4

You know the drill, don't skip over this section! Stop for just a few minutes to reflect on what you've read and what you can recall, all in service of retaining the learning.

Here are some questions for you to write the answers to:

➡ What do you recall from this chapter?
➡ What rings true to you?
➡ What do you see more clearly now?
➡ How does this feel in your body?
➡ What else do you sense?
➡ Which mindsets do you want to discard to make way for more transformational mindsets?
➡ What else did your work instil in you that you could discard to be a more masterful coach?

Habit change commitment 4

It's time to commit to trying something different, based on what has resonated with you. This template will help you to make *one* commitment to make *one* small change. When you're comfortable with that, you can make another, and another.

➡ Instead of believing the voice in my head that says...
➡ Which leads me to do/say...
➡ I choose to believe...
➡ And will therefore do/say...
➡ My cue or reminder is...
➡ My immediate reward will be...

You may choose to share this commitment with a coaching buddy for more social accountability.

Now, stop reading and writing: go and experiment with what you have learned, before coming back for more mindset shifts in the rest of the book.

Chapter 5

Mindsets we learned from managers that we need to discard to be a more masterful coach

As if we didn't learn enough from work and organisational life, our managers will have had an influence on how we think, feel and act. Each of our managers will have had distinct work ethics that they'll have expected us to adhere to, certain ways of communicating and different expectations in general. If we wanted to fit in and be ranked highly, we might have moulded ourselves to their ways of working. They'll each have had their own motivations that drove their spoken and unspoken ground rules. And if you've been a manager yourself, you'll also have developed philosophies and principles that have shaped you to become the person you are today.

As you think about the messages that your managers imparted in the way they spoke and acted, what did they teach you that you have needed to discard to be a more masterful coach? And as you think about yourself, if you were ever in that role, what did you believe in that role that you have needed to discard to be a more masterful coach?

🐾 Shift 49

OLD MINDSET: You work for me
NEW MINDSET: We work together

In a boss–employee relationship, there's an inherent power differential. If I use the word 'subordinate' in place of employee, it's even more obvious. The boss has power over the employee, and as an employee, we usually learn to play that power-under role. Respecting our superior. Doing the work that our supervisor needs us to do. Following the leader's lead.

In coaching, our relationship must be a relationship of equals. The power differential needs to disappear. As we've touched on previously, this can be tricky if we use words such as 'coachee' to describe the thinker. The '-ee' denotes something being done to the coachee, that they're on the receiving end of coaching and diminutive (Benjamin 2017). That's partly why I like Nancy Kline's (2002) term 'thinker' to describe them. Again as we've seen, a thinker holds the power and agency to think for themselves.

But thinkers may sometimes approach coaching as though you, the coach, are their superior. They give away their power to you, seeing you as the expert or the one to whom they should defer. This can be a symptom of their employed upbringing. If you pick up that mantle of power, equality and partnership are lost.

As a coach, you must start as you mean to continue, shepherding the process of creating a partnership, where you:

➡ both have a say about whether you are a good fit to work together
➡ contract together to co-create a thinking environment that works for you both, including boundaries around cancellation, no-shows, lateness, completion, etc.
➡ use 'we' language rather than 'I and you' when you are discussing your ways of working, e.g. 'How shall we do this work together today?'
➡ ask them what they think you need to cover together, where they want to start and go next, what would be most valuable to them,

what they are taking away, rather than making those decisions for them

➡ are unattached to anything that you offer – a question, an observation, a piece of feedback – accepting their response, whatever that is and letting go of your need to prove yourself

➡ take responsibility for the process (with the thinker's input), while the thinker takes responsibility for the thinking

➡ keep yourself organised, while they keep themselves organised and on track

➡ stand side-by-side with them, without any sense of knowing best, curious about what they notice

➡ acknowledge their beliefs, values and progress rather than praising them, which is judgemental and holds power (see also Shifts 7 and 25).

Coach and thinker are equals, not superior and inferior, not knowing and unknowing. All these aspects of partnership allow you to share power and responsibility. You'll need to hold yourself to account for staying in an 'Adult' space, inviting the thinker into that same space (Berne 1964), so that they can fully account for themselves rather than discounting themselves – 'discounting' in this case defined by Schiff et al. (1975) as 'to minimise or ignore some aspect of themselves' and losing their power.

Modelling that adult-to-adult relationship here will be useful to them in all other walks of their life.

✦ Shift 50

OLD MINDSET: The boss says jump, you say: 'How high?'

NEW MINDSET: We talk about both our needs

The expression: 'When I say jump, you say, "how high?"' was something I saw played out repeatedly in my previous corporate life. Hierarchy trumped discussion. I'm guessing that at some point, people who did speak up had their heads bitten off (to a greater or lesser degree) and stopped speaking up. That could have been about ideas they had, different ways of approaching something, different work patterns that they wanted to carve out for themselves – you name it. If bosses tell us 'no' as a pattern, we stop asking or recommending or discussing alternatives, and sooner or later we vote with our feet by walking out of the organisation.

You might have inherited this same way of being when you became a coach: the thinker asks you to jump, you ask how high. The power dynamic here is the reverse of what I described in the previous mindset (see Shift 49). The thinker holds the power, demanding that we serve them. This reflects the consumer mentality that we talked about in Shift 38: 'I (the thinker) am paying for this, so you (the coach) will do my bidding.' (I'm exaggerating for effect here!)

But as we saw in Shift 38, coaches are not service providers, despite the money that changes hands. We're a partner, creating a space for thinkers to do their best thinking. Our role is to create the thinking environment; theirs is to do the thinking.

Coach and thinker both have needs here. The thinker wants to move forward in their quest for a better life. The coach wants to feel fulfilled in enabling the thinker to move forward in that quest *and* the coach needs to stay sane and earn a living while doing that. You may have other needs too, which it would behove you to identify, so you can voice those needs as you contract with each thinker.

To feel fulfilled, I know that I need the thinker to be prepared to work hard at the thinking and moving forward. As mentioned previously, I may need to nudge them into that, but ultimately it's up to them to come prepared to think and make their own progress.

We've also seen that to earn a living, you need some boundaries in place around cancellation, no-shows, lateness and endings. You'll decide what those boundaries are, and your choices have consequences for those earnings. These boundaries also help you keep your sanity (see Shifts 2 and 48).

To stay sane, coach and thinker also need to share responsibility. Your responsibility is for the process; the thinker's is for the thinking and moving forward. This isn't a 50/50 responsibility, as we aren't parsing out the same responsibilities between us. Again, your responsibility is for the process; the thinker's is for the thinking and moving forward. You each take 100 per cent responsibility for your part.

You also invest in supervision to enable you to resource yourself, and maintain your sanity.

Your needs are as important as each thinker's needs. The more explicitly you discuss both sets of needs, the more likely you are to work in ways that serve you both.

In summary, the ICF has a set of useful guidelines for the beginning of a new coaching relationship, encouraging us to:

➡ 'explain what coaching is and isn't and describe the process to the client and relevant stakeholders
➡ reach agreement about what is and isn't appropriate in the relationship, what is and isn't being offered, and the responsibilities of the client and relevant stakeholders
➡ reach agreement about the guidelines and specific parameters of the coaching relationship, such as logistics, fees, scheduling, duration, termination, confidentiality and inclusion of others
➡ partner with [the thinker] and relevant stakeholders to establish an overall coaching plan and goals
➡ partner with [the thinker] to determine [thinker]–coach compatibility'. (ICF 2019)

☁ Shift 51

OLD MINDSET: Come with solutions, not questions

NEW MINDSET: Be OK with not knowing

Here's another of those sayings that emanate so frequently from managers' mouths: 'Come to me with solutions, not problems or questions.' It's meant to be positive for both parties. First, the manager wants you to think it through for yourself, so they don't have to do all the heavy lifting. Second, they think that gives you, the employee, the chance to build your own thinking muscles and grow into yourself as a result.

The problem with this is that it's hard to think in your own head. Much more beneficial, if not always linear, is to think and process out loud. By telling us to come with solutions already figured out, a manager is disabling that thinking-out-loud function. Solutions may be half-cooked, raw, unpalatable.

Employees don't want the opposite either – a manager who gives the answers. That doesn't stretch them at all; in fact, it makes them lazy. The more the person asks their manager what to do, the more that person continues to ask their manager what to do because the manager's answers disable the individual from thinking for themselves.

Managers might think they can't win – but they can, if they ask questions. Not leading questions that have an in-built solution, but curious ones that don't hold the recipe. Questions that create new ways of thinking. It's like inventing a new recipe that has never been created before.

This is what the coach needs to infuse into their coaching: not knowing the answers, and not even knowing the question until the moment it is needed. An infusion suggests that something is present, though – when nothing is present except our presence. Not problem solving on behalf of the thinker. Not cooking the recipe for them. Not even having a recipe in the first place. Rather, co-creating a new recipe by coming into the coaching space in a state of not knowing.

If you listen to that manager's voice saying, 'Come [to coaching] with solutions,' you'll have a hard time with this state of not knowing – as you'll approach coaching in a state of knowing. If you listen to a different voice saying: 'Approach coaching with a blank sheet of paper, without paint or implements or water,' you'll embrace this state of not knowing more confidently (see also Shifts 27 and 40).

⧗ Shift 52

OLD MINDSET: Knowledge is power
NEW MINDSET: The coach's knowledge is limited

Sir Francis Bacon first coined the phrase 'knowledge itself is power' in 1597. He likely meant that having and sharing knowledge enables us to achieve more, and so builds our reputation, influence and power. He sees it as a positive.

You may have had managers or mentors in the past who quoted this phrase to encourage you to embrace learning and knowledge, read, network and study. They also saw it as positive – and you can see why. Knowing more can help you to solve more problems.

That's a good thing, right?

Partly right.

If we look at it another way, the more we know, the more others defer to us. We become bigger, and they become smaller by comparison. It could be somewhat Machiavellian: cunning, scheming, unscrupulous. (We've examined the imbalance of power in Shifts 5, 38, 49 and 50.)

As coaches, we need to let go of the need to know more, learn more techniques, have more tools in our toolkit. These can get in the way if they lead the thinker to feel that power imbalance – of our knowing in comparison to their not knowing. You're not striving for power anyway, and knowing *an* answer isn't necessarily the most *useful* answer for the thinker.

Your knowledge is limited. You can never know enough about them, their culture, personality, beliefs, values and desires to come up with a perfect solution: they know these better than anyone in the world could possibly do so, and their knowledge and wisdom are all there within them.

That is the knowledge that's bountiful: your job is to pull it out from within them. It's not to pour your limited knowing into them.

Your not knowing can be more useful than knowing. The knowing will come, but not to you; it will come to the thinker as they work things out for themselves. When they join their own dots and create their own meaning, that's when knowledge is power. They'll step into their own potent power, as they will own their answers and new knowing.

♨ Shift 53

OLD MINDSET: Think like me
NEW MINDSET: Challenge my assumptions

It's not uncommon at work for us to start to think like our manager or other people around us. We fall into a state of what Janis (1972) calls 'groupthink'. This is partly self-preservation – the more we think like our manager, the more they'll take our ideas on board and the better they'll rate us. Baumeister and Leary (1995) show us that it's partly about belonging – we want to feel part of the tribe. We feel a need to blend, self-censor, fit in. There may be external pressure from the manager to think in the same way, too. We may reduce our levels of decisional stress by agreeing quickly.

It's little wonder that we listen to the explicit or implicit voice of a manager to think like them. We are drawn towards groupthink – and collusion.

This isn't useful in coaching. Your role is to challenge the thinker's assumptions; to shine a light on their 'blind spots'; to enable them to think for themselves about what they believe, not what others believe.

I was listening to a recording of a coach coaching a thinker a few months back, in which the thinker's father's voice loomed large. The thinker was listening to her father's opinion and had made herself subservient to it. Her father was obviously important to her, and she clearly respected his point of view, but so much so that she had lost herself to it, lost her own perspective. She was thinking like him.

The coach's role in this circumstance is to draw out the much quieter voice of the thinker, to make it louder so that first this voice could be heard, then acknowledged, then embraced if felt useful to do so. Instead, the coach let the thinker (and her father) off the hook, and worked at a more transactional level.

The coach was colluding in the assumption that the thinker should pay attention to her father's voice, rather than listening to her own needs. Maybe this was partly driven by the coach's relationship with her own father or a previous manager – perhaps she recognised it and saw it as normal, so passed over it.

If what the thinker says resonates with you, perhaps because you have faced something similar, you can end up colluding and not checking in on assumptions. If the culture they work in is similar to a culture that you have worked in, you may not challenge the way they think about that culture or the norms within it. You might play the same game with them that this is how it's always been, so this is how it will always be. That doesn't serve them either.

Sometimes it's your voice that becomes too loud, prevalent or forceful. The thinker may defer to you, make themselves small in your shadow or put you on a pedestal. It can come from either party – making yourself too big, or the thinker making you big. This may be 'think like me' residue.

➡ Do you notice even a minuscule amount of this in you?
➡ What are the assumptions that you hold?
➡ Where do you see yourself colluding with thinkers' assumptions?
➡ Which assumptions do you need to challenge in yourself, and in the thinkers with whom you partner?

⚛ Shift 54

Managers often feel pressure to know all the answers to all the questions that their employees might ask. That is a high and (dare I say it) an impossible bar to aspire to: none of us has all the answers in this day and age of fast-paced change.

Here's what I see happening. An employee asks their manager what to do in a situation. Said manager feels the pressure to have all the answers and/or to move decisions on quickly, so gives an answer. This is a good short-term fix, as the employee can go away and act (maybe, if they actually understand the answer fully), and the manager gets to go back to their work.

But it keeps happening. The same employee comes back with similar or additional questions. They get into a habit of feeling that they should ask permission rather than forgiveness. The amount of time the manager spends on decision making just keeps on increasing.

Why can't the employee figure it out for themselves, the manager wonders?

'They're not new anymore; they should know what to do after all the answers I've given them! I never get around to doing the more strategic thinking that I need to, as I'm always helping my team members. I'm feeling unfulfilled and under-challenged.'

Sound familiar?

At the same time, the employee feels equally unfulfilled, as they just do what they're told. They don't have to think, but that's leaving them feeling under-challenged.

Both manager and employee are in the same position, unfulfilled, under-challenged, not able to operate at the level for which they are paid. It's a vicious cycle dragging them both down. The more the manager answers the questions about decisions the employee could make for themselves, the more the employee will come back with more questions, and so it continues.

But it could be different. There is another way.

It takes just one small tweak on the part of the manager.

If you're a coach you will recognise this, but sometimes you might be carrying the vestiges of being this manager previously, or used to telling people what to do in other circumstances.

Here's the tweak: ask them what they think about the situation and the possible resolutions and consequences. Put the question back to them. Yes, you might need to ask a series of questions, and that might take a bit longer than telling them what to do. But in the long term, they'll stop asking you and start asking themselves.

Stop blaming the thinker for asking you what you would do: you are perpetuating that behaviour by answering those questions, making their brains lazy. Look to yourself and how you can change that one small behaviour to enable them to change theirs.

Are you falling into the trap as a coach of providing thinkers with answers when they hook you in with their questions?

It's time to break the habit, but first shift your mindset.

 Shift 55

> **OLD MINDSET: Feedback is painful**
> **NEW MINDSET: Objective feedback is useful**

As a manager or team member, you may have felt that giving constructive feedback was a painful part of the job. So painful, in fact, that you avoided it. You might not have wanted to be critical, fearing that you might hurt the other person's feelings. Or fearing conflict and pushback about your own contribution to the situation.

That may be stopping you from giving feedback as a coach, and yet this is part of the role. Not performance feedback, of course, as that's the role of their manager who is with them every day and responsible for holding them to account for progress and the way they go about that.

This is a different kind of feedback, about how you experience them in relationship with you.

Why is this important? Because the way the thinker shows up in relationship with you is likely to be representative of the way they show up in other relationships. Whereas others may never have had the courage to give them feedback, you are in a perfect position to offer it from a place of compassion.

This may still feel difficult, but if you learn how to give objective, evidence-based feedback, it can be heard and received as useful. When we talk about feedback, that can be positive as well as constructive. What is objective feedback?

→ It's neutral, without judgement. Not 'I like the way you...', or 'I love the way you...' Even though these are positive, they are still judgemental. Better to say: 'I notice how you...', 'I saw you do X', 'I heard you say...'. These are all actual observations of behaviour.

→ It's based on a benchmark of some kind. That might be a set of leadership competencies that the organisation has developed, the coaching goals or the stated values of the organisation or the individual.

➡ It is succinct, without waffle or sales pitch, both of which water it down.

➡ It is supportive *and* challenging. Sometimes positive, sometimes constructive – but don't get caught in the 'praise sandwich', which again waters it down (Bressler et al. 2014). Keep them separate.

➡ It comes from a place of wanting them to succeed, not willing them to fail.

➡ It is not minimised, for example: 'This is just a small thing, but...'

It may sound something like:

➡ 'One of your coaching goals is to X [e.g. to be more succinct in your communications]. I notice how you do Y [e.g. I notice that you have been talking for 15 minutes] here in this coaching space. Of course, this is a safe space where you can be yourself, *and* I wonder how that is representative of what we are working on?'

➡ 'When you say X/do Y, I experience you as Z. I wonder what feedback you have received from others about this?'

➡ 'When you say X/do Y, I notice myself doing/feeling Z. I wonder how that might be representative of the way you show up in other relationships and what the impact of that might be?'

This is being direct, not directive. Being useful in that directness. Being challenging within the context of the supportive relationship you have developed together.

🧠 Shift 56

OLD MINDSET: Why?
NEW MINDSET: What and how?

Managers often find themselves asking why something happened, why someone chose the path they did, why something wasn't finished. You may recognise yourself in that if you've ever been a manager, or you may recognise it from some of the managers with whom you worked.

The trouble with 'why' questions is that they put the other person on the defensive, rationalising themselves or their decisions. It can feel like blame is being ladled out, or that the manager thinks the decision was wrong. The other person ends up justifying, explaining, going back over old ground.

I hear some coaches asking 'why' without realising what it can do to the thinker. They don't always notice the flicker of resistance to the question, or the distance it creates between the two of them.

Explore with them, don't inadvertently accuse.

Questions that start with 'what' and 'how' are much more likely to elicit new thinking, rather than self-protective thinking. At the beginning of a session, these might be questions such as:

➡ 'What is most useful to think about today?'
➡ 'What is important to you about that?' (You see how this is a 'why' question, but softened to avoid defensiveness.)
➡ 'What is your specific question for our X minutes?'
➡ 'How will you know you have got what you need from this session?'
➡ 'What do we need to cover in order to get you to that place today?'
➡ 'How would you like us to work together on that?'

In the middle, those 'what' and 'how' questions might be along these lines:

➡ 'How does it feel in your body as you say that?'
➡ 'What is the meaning of X [a word they have used] to you?'
➡ 'What is important to you about Y?'

➡ 'What is the connection between X and Y for you?'
➡ 'How does that reflect on what you want to work on today?'

  – or something in your own words.
  And at the back end of a coaching session:

➡ 'What are your intended results?'
➡ 'What challenges do you anticipate?'
➡ 'What have you learned from previous projects that might be useful here?'
➡ 'What will enable you to succeed this time?'

'When', 'where' and 'with whom' questions are more useful at this back end too, to pin the thinker down to their self-identified next steps. Using these questions earlier is more likely to elicit information for the coach, rather than new thinking or commitment for the thinker.

When you're listening to recordings of your coaching, listen out for 'why' questions and see what subtle changes they cause. I suspect this will persuade you to stop yourself in your tracks next time, and ask a 'what' or a 'how' question instead.

✍ Shift 57

OLD MINDSET: Always be professional
NEW MINDSET: Show your human credentials

As I was interviewing people about habits that get in the way of great coaching, this one came up from a former human resources manager who had later retrained as a coach: she always felt as though she had to be unemotional and professional in all her conversations with the people in her business.

Other people I interviewed concurred. There's an expectation of professionalism in a business context. This might differ from one organisation to another, but it's likely to consist of:

➡ competence
➡ knowledge
➡ conscientiousness
➡ integrity (being true to our word)
➡ respect for others (including timekeeping in respect of others' precious time)
➡ emotional intelligence (including how we speak to others)
➡ appropriateness (around dress, grooming, body language, what you discuss at work, the way you speak and write for your context)
➡ confidence
➡ needing to be flawless.

You could argue that every coach needs all these too (except knowledge of what's being brought to coaching – see Shifts 27 and 40 – and being flawless). But if these hide the true, authentic you, the thinker will notice a mismatch. They want to know you are human too, that you and your life aren't perfect. Not that you should be wearing your heart on your sleeve, but talking about the coaching you have for yourself, for example, shows them that you are still a work-in-progress – just as they are.

ICF Competency 4.6 around trust and safety says that a coach shows openness and transparency as a way to display vulnerability and build trust with the client – so there you have it.

I notice how sharing our own story in the chemistry session can affect the thinker's decision to move forward into coaching with us. For example, telling them something of the obstacles we have overcome in the past, such as bereavement, mental ill-health or redundancy. This shows us as vulnerable, just as they are, with a soft underbelly. Brené Brown (2015) found in her research that admitting to our vulnerabilities shows up as a strength to others.

I noticed this the other day when I shared a client challenge I was facing with a group of supervisees. One of them said: 'That makes me feel so much better, to know that even a supervisor has challenges.' Yes, I do – I'm not up on a pedestal with all the answers. I'm working my way through the maze of learning as well.

I find this helps us to partner better, as we become equalised in our vulnerability. The thinker stops giving us all their power, and we stop taking power. We're looking at this together, side-by-side, not knowing what will emerge.

What other human credentials might you display to build trust and safety?

Laughing together. Being touched by their learning. Showing support, empathy and concern (PCC Marker 4.2).

Being open about your family make-up on your website or social media posts. Telling funny, sad or difficult stories about your non-work life on social media. Being honest about the ups and downs.

Create a niche from the obstacles that you've overcome yourself: for example, as we've seen previously, branding yourself as the introvert's coach, as you are an introvert and have learned how to be your best. Or the retirement coach who's approaching semi-retirement. Or the coach working with women in a man's world, as they have done themselves in the past.

Your story is part and parcel of this niche.

How else do you show your human credentials?

🤝 Shift 58

OLD MINDSET: People are not resourceful
NEW MINDSET: People can figure it out with support

Did you ever have a manager who thought everyone else was stupid? Maybe they weren't as explicit as that, but you could tell they thought that their way was the best and only way to go about something, and nobody else had it in them to make things work. They didn't recognise how resourceful people can be if they have the right support to access that resourcefulness.

In coaching, we look through an entirely different lens.

Everyone is 'creative, resourceful and whole' (Whitworth et al. 1998). They can figure it out, and sometimes need a little nudge to do so: a question here, an observation there. Support to dig deeper. A belief in their ability to think, feel and be. A belief that they can access strengths that enable them to be more than they ever dreamt possible.

All of this is underpinned by the Pygmalion effect (Rosenthal and Jacobson 1968). According to this research, people internalise the labels they're given, whether positive or negative. People act according to those expectations, so creating a self-fulfilling prophecy. If we believe that someone is unresourceful and treat them as such, they will become unresourceful. If we believe they're resourceful and support them to be so, they will become resourceful. This isn't always the case, as some people rebel against expectations to prove a point; but in coaching, we rely on this effect hugely.

The thing is, you can't simply say that you believe the thinker to be 'creative, resourceful and whole'. You need to follow that through with word and deed – with everyone. You need to be sure that your unconscious biases (for example, about those who are neurodiverse) do not switch off this belief in their capacity to think for themselves.

For example, if you give the thinker ideas and solutions, that's highlighting that you don't think they are resourceful – they might stop thinking for themselves, and prove you right.

☝ Shift 59

Some managers or mentors think they know what's best for the people working with them.

I had a mentor in my early career who kept talking about me becoming the first female CEO of the bank I worked for, and all the things I needed to do at that early stage in my career to make that a reality.

He thought that would be good for me (and presumably good for his reputation too, as my mentor). I admire him for wanting such a thing for me, the bank and society.

But it wasn't what I wanted. It wasn't good for me at all.

This mentor didn't disguise his advice, but some coaches disguise theirs within questions. The questions lead to answers that are seen to be 'good for' the thinker, according to the coach's measures of success.

But what about the thinker's measures of success? What do they want from a career or for their life?

I recall a colleague telling me the story of a talent forum that discussed placing a high-flier into a new country to run the operations there. The forum presumed this would be 'good for' the person.

But it couldn't have been further from what the individual wanted for himself and his family. A move halfway across the world to a place where they didn't speak the language, taking the children away from their schools and friends? No thank you! The talent forum had never asked – they had just assumed that this 'amazing' opportunity would appeal to anyone and everyone who was tapped on the shoulder.

You can't presume that you know what is good for the people you work with in coaching. They know what will be good for them, or at least a step towards better – if you give them a chance to figure it out by asking unloaded questions.

Coaches know this, and yet they still do it. I see it frequently as I observe them: they don't always realise that they are doing it. They might be asking questions that start with:

➡ 'Have you thought of...?'
➡ 'Will you [insert suggestion]...?'
➡ 'What about...?'

Yes, these are questions, but they're also advice disguised as questions. It's as though the coach knows the best answer for the thinker. Yet there could be a hundred alternative ways forward if we sit with not knowing and allow the thinker to figure out their own advice and answers.

⬛ Shift 60

OLD MINDSET: I need to produce and send written notes

NEW MINDSET: Thinkers are adults and can capture their learning in words that are true to them

If you've ever chaired a meeting in or outside of work, you may have learned to produce and send written notes as a record of the decisions in that meeting – or to have a minute-taker to do that on everyone's behalf.

This is useful in that setting. It gives the meeting attendees something to go back to, to check on what was agreed, who is doing what, what the deadlines are, etc.; it's often a way of holding people accountable to action.

But if we transfer this note-taking to the coaching arena, it's as though we become the personal assistant to the thinker. It's a service, not the act of a partner (see also Shifts 5, 38, 49 and 50).

We undermine the thinker's ability to take responsibility for keeping their own notes. As we've seen throughout this book, they are adults. They decide whether to take notes or not. If they find it distracting to make notes while thinking, we can contract for a pause part-way through the session for them to capture what they have learned, and again at the end – whatever works for them. Another alternative we've already identified is for them to record the session, so that they can listen back.

The way you would capture a summary isn't the way they would capture it for themselves anyway. Your words and interpretations are not theirs. What you capture will not necessarily be the most important aspects for them. You may miss or overemphasise something.

This is taking too much responsibility. It's parental. It's infantilising and disempowering.

You may push back and say: 'Well, if I'm going to write notes for myself, why wouldn't I send them out to the thinker as well? It's no more work.' But why are you keeping this level of notes in the first place? To check back on their progress in the next session, to hold them accountable? Again, this is parental behaviour. You need to help them to hold themselves accountable, or to find people in their immediate surroundings who can, so they don't become dependent on you to do that.

We've seen in previous shifts that where they start from in the next session may be streets ahead of where they ended the last one. Why would you take them back there when so much will be different? You don't need this kind of note-taking for yourself either (see also Shift 21).

Retrieval practice 5

Here we are again, at retrieval practice. Stop for just a few minutes to reflect on what you've read and what you can recall, all in service of retaining the learning.

Here are some questions for you to write the answers to:

➡ What do you recall from this chapter?
➡ What rings true to you?
➡ What do you see more clearly now?
➡ How does this feel in your body?
➡ What else do you sense?
➡ Which mindsets do you want to discard to make way for more transformational mindsets?
➡ What else did your managers instil in you that you could discard to be a more masterful coach?

Habit change commitment 5

It's time to commit to trying something different, based on what has resonated with you. This template will help you to make *one* commitment to make *one* small change. When you're comfortable with that, you can make another, and another.

➡ Instead of believing the voice in my head that says...
➡ Which leads me to do/say...
➡ I choose to believe...
➡ And will therefore do/say...
➡ My cue or reminder is...
➡ My immediate reward will be...

You may choose to share this commitment with a coaching buddy for more social accountability.

Now, stop reading and writing: go and experiment with what you have learned, before coming back for more mindset shifts in the rest of the book.

Chapter 6

Mindsets we learned from our coach training that we need to discard to be a more masterful coach

You might imagine that your coach training would have taught you only good habits. That's mostly true, but when I observe coaches there are a few things I notice that have come from their training that need to be discarded. Some of it might be unintentional on the part of the training company, a symptom of the way the training is set up perhaps, rather than explicitly taught content. (I'm not having a go at coach training companies, just shining a light on some aspects that could be addressed at this early stage of the formation of a coach.)

Before you dig in, what did you learn at your coach training that you have subsequently changed for the better in your coaching?

⛨ Shift 61

OLD MINDSET: The work happens when we are together

NEW MINDSET: The work happens when we are apart

I observe coaches trying to complete everything in the coaching session, as though the thinker cannot do anything alone without them. Somehow in our coach training, we learn, perhaps implicitly, that the coaching session is where everything happens. Perhaps this is simply because we are learning how to conduct a coaching session, and don't really talk much about what happens outside of it?

It's as though all the work has to happen when coach and thinker are together, otherwise the coach has failed the thinker. This shows up in action-oriented questions too early in the session, driving to get to a solution to what the thinker brought to coaching, running over time to finish what has been started, or pushing for a complete session (whatever 'complete' is, see also Shifts 15 and 23).

We're kidding ourselves if we think that the thinker can only think when we are with them. I would go further than that, and say we're allowing our ego to get too big for its boots. We're no longer working as an equal if we believe they're inadequate outside the session. They're 'creative, resourceful and whole' (Whitworth et al. 1998) in and *out* of the session; we can't allow our ego to disempower them and disable their potential.

So much happens in between sessions. For a start, the thinker usually puts into practice what they decided to experiment with: that's the real work, testing out whether their ideas are successful in practice, and trying something different if it isn't successful. That's why your session close is so important, to ensure the thinker has figured out:

➡ what to experiment with
➡ what support they can call on – internal and external
➡ what obstacles might get in their way, and how they will get

around them

➤ what they hope to learn as a result (see also Shifts 17 and 79 about CLOSE).

But it's more than them taking action. Their subconscious – or perhaps their conscious – will carry on thinking about the things you mulled over together in the session. Maybe a question that they avoided within the session has stuck with them, and they keep coming back to it. Or maybe they had an acorn of an idea that they continue to grow in between sessions. Or maybe it's simply a case of getting more of what you focus on. This will happen over time, *and* you can encourage the thinker to take time out straight after the session to continue to reflect. If they dash off to their next meeting immediately, they will lose out on a huge amount of continuous processing.

When I'm the thinker, I'm often surprised when I look back at my intentions before a follow-up session and realise how much progress I've made, even without conscious effort. Perhaps I've had more conversations with others in the meantime, which led to a deeper understanding. And sometimes that conscious effort *is* necessary to break old habits and replace them with new ones.

That's the hard work of making change.

I know that not all thinkers follow through on their promises to themselves, but that doesn't mean they're inadequate without you. Perhaps the two of you hadn't got to the root cause for the thinker to figure out a fitting way forward, or hadn't surfaced the belief that was getting in the way of change, or something more important or urgent came up that trumped the thinker's intentions.

That doesn't mean that they can only do the work in the session, with you. You can't be with them all the time, and your job is to enable them to act independently of you, drawing on their own internal resources and others around them. The work happens outside of the session.

⬆SHIFT Shift 62

OLD MINDSET: Change happens after the session

NEW MINDSET: Get the shift in the room by doing it now

This might seem contradictory to the last Shift, where the work happens when we're apart. It's important to get the shift in the room *and* know that the work continues when we are apart.

We may assume that coach and thinker talk *in* the session, and the thinker does something different to change *after* the session. If you believe your job is to get them to *talk* in the session and *do* after it, you are missing potential opportunities to support them in their shift.

I see a connection here to Kolb's (1984) learning cycle and Honey and Mumford's (1986) learning styles, which found that we each have a preference for learning:

➡ by doing – 'the activist'
➡ through reflection – 'the reflector'
➡ through theory and models – 'the theorist'
➡ by experimentation – 'the pragmatist'.

They also found that the best learning draws on all four of these, no matter where we start, going around the whole cycle.

Perhaps you think your job as coach is to get thinkers into a place of reflective observation in the session. Maybe you've learned that active experimentation only happens outside of the session, with concrete experience following hot on its heels. But to me, and to Hawkins and Smith (2011), who said, 'Get the shift in the room', it's important to bring that active experimentation forward so you can support them in that first run-through and enable them to embody the change – really feel it somatically, rather than just talk about it.

If they embody the change, it's like a practice run. Their body and mind know they've done it once before and, according to my own research for my master's dissertation (Norman 1999), this makes it easier to do a second and third time because we know we can. It's in the muscle memory. You're enabling the thinker to believe in themselves and their capacity to change.

For example, if they're talking about a conversation they intend to have with their manager, you can invite them to practise the first sentence or two of what they wish to say as though they're saying it to their manager – and ideally standing in a different place to where they have been thinking about it, so their body knows this is no longer reflecting, but now experimenting. They might play with it in this safe environment until it feels authentic and fitting for the situation. If they only talk about it, they won't feel the same level of confidence as they go into the conversation, as they won't know exactly how it will sound when it comes out of their mouth that first time; neither would they have experienced it in their body.

Another time when doing it now can be useful is when the thinker says something along the lines of: 'I'll sit down and write a list after the session,' or 'My next step is to work on this spreadsheet'. I invite them to do that now, right there in the session, if that would be a useful way for them to use our time together. I can be with them, silently giving them my attention in service of them capturing their ideas, or they can choose to use the time to work alone. If the latter, we'll agree to come back at the end of our time together to wrap up – or we might wrap up at this point and they get on with it alone.

This may be the best use of your time together, even if you don't feel as though you're doing anything. You are doing something – holding the space for them to work on what matters most to them in this moment, and getting the shift into the room. Their action evokes more awareness and progress. That momentum that they get in the room, breaking the back of the list, spreadsheet, mind map or whatever, is more likely to keep the momentum going after the session.

🗞️ Shift 63

OLD MINDSET: We must understand today's reality

NEW MINDSET: Today's reality is only useful if it is new thinking

If your training taught you the GROW model (Goals, Reality, Options, Way Forward), you might be wondering how the mindset of interrupting storytelling (see Shift 4) relates to the R of GROW: Reality.

John Whitmore (2012) suggested that coaches should ask questions that get to an understanding of the current reality: but that is usually well known to the thinker; it takes them into familiar territory. This means the questions in this phase of GROW are often about filling the coach in on that reality, rather than filling the thinker in on new thinking.

Coach beware! As we've seen previously, you might be using too much of the time to fill yourself in, asking information-gathering questions, and not enough on getting to new thinking.

That said, the ICF (2019) does have a PCC Marker that encourages coaches to ask 'questions about the client, such as their current way of thinking, feeling, values, needs, wants, beliefs or behaviour' (PCC Marker 7.1). Yes, those questions are about the *current* way of thinking, but you will notice that the questions aren't about the problem, they're about the person, as Marion Franklin (2019) and Marcia Reynolds (2020) put it. This is much more about the 'who' than the 'what' – not about the story. These 'who' questions take the thinker vertically and deeper to understanding themselves better rather than gathering data about the situation.

The ICF (2019) goes on to encourage us to ask 'questions to help the client explore beyond the client's current thinking or feeling to new or expanded ways of thinking or feeling about themself' (PCC Marker 7.2) and 'about their situation' (PCC Marker 7.3). Your role is to support and challenge new thinking and feeling about themselves or the situation, rather than dwelling on the current thinking or feeling. Exploring underneath the thinker's surface, rather than exploring the story, chronology, players or context that the thinker already knows.

⇄ Shift 64

OLD MINDSET: What have you tried already?
NEW MINDSET: When you think about things you have tried already, what have you learned?

'What have you tried already?' is not a question that creates new thinking. It goes over old ground. It is filling in the coach rather than filling in the thinker. It might even lead to justification or explanation about why those things didn't work. These can dig a thinker deeper into a mindset of 'Nothing works, I might as well give up now – I've tried everything I can think of'.

I never quite understood why training schools teach this question. Maybe it relates to the Reality part of the GROW model (if that's the model you were taught).

There's a glimmer of something useful in the idea of checking on what they have tried already – and that something could be about what they learned from trying those things, without going into the story of what they did. This could be useful in moving them into fresh territory and new ideas.

The better question, then, is: 'When you think about things you have tried in the past, what have you learned?' Or other questions that come from a similar place, but draw on successes:

➡ 'What can you learn from times in the past when you have succeeded in this?'
➡ 'If you think about times when you have [overcome this barrier], what transferable skills can you apply in this situation?'

You can see how these questions are much more future-focused, positive and presuppositional. By presuppositional, I mean that the questions presume there *are* learning and transferable skills, so enabling the thinker to access them.

Try them: see what a difference they make to the quality of the new thinking and mood.

📷 Shift 65

OLD MINDSET: Face-to-face is best
NEW MINDSET: Virtual is just as powerful

Historically, many coach training courses were face-to-face – so we learned to coach like this. That might give us the impression that this is the only way – or the best way. The training company may not have explicitly said that, but that's the experience we receive and the conclusion we draw. The chances are you might have practised in between sessions on the phone or online, learning to coach virtually as well. But did you ever stop to think about the relative merits of face-to-face and virtual coaching?

I look at the world through an 'experience' lens: customer, employee, leader. What's the best coaching experience I can provide for the leaders I coach? When I apply the experience lens to virtual coaching, the answer may surprise you.

Leaders are hyper-busy. They want space to think about those things that are important but not urgent, for which they don't give themselves time to strategise. I want to support them to do their best thinking, and I notice that when a leader is in their own space – a place where they feel safe – they can be more vulnerable and honest, both with themselves and me. I recommend that they not be in their office, as those walls seem to keep them tied to their old ways of thinking, but rather to choose a space that enables them to feel resourceful and creative.

Many people assume that face-to-face coaching must be better than virtual coaching. A study by Berry et al. (2011) found 'no difference in the reported level of problem-resolution for face-to-face and distance clients'. The strength of the working alliance was found to be significant for problem-resolution in distance coaching, and 'coaches self-reported strong levels of working alliance in both conditions (face-to-face and distance)'.

Another study, published in 2011 in the *British Journal of Psychology*, found that:

Gaze aversion benefits cognitive performance, not just by disengaging visual attention from irrelevant visual information, but also by interrupting social interaction processes involved in face-to-face communication. (Markson and Paterson 2009)

This suggests that the coaching experience is better for thinkers when there is no need for eye contact. Coaching where the coach and thinker are walking side by side, are on the telephone or have disabled both webcams meets that need.

The leaders I work with are often in global companies, working virtually with their peers and team members. They're used to virtual conversations, even though they often feel they don't do them well. For leaders working in a virtual (and now hybrid) world, virtual coaching provides an added benefit of modelling great virtual conversations.

Through this experience, they can learn how to:

➡ contract for a successful conversation
➡ engage their people in decent-quality, engaging conversations that build independent, critical thinkers and decision makers
➡ close a conversation well.

You're missing an opportunity when you coach leaders face-to-face, if that isn't the world in which they normally operate.

Silence is your greatest gift to the thinker, and it takes practice over the phone to know when they've finished their thinking. Being fully present, without the overwhelm of face-to-face distractions, allows you to access your somatic intelligence. For example, it can be powerful to offer up to a thinker that your chest has suddenly tightened (or whatever you are feeling in your body), and ask them whether that offers any insights.

Active listening also allows you to hear what is unsaid. According to Kraus (2017), 'across five experiments, individuals who only listened without observing were able, on average, to identify more accurately the emotions being experienced by others'. This tells us just how powerful audio-only coaching can be.

Without visual clues, you need to home in on listening between the lines even more, paying attention to every breath, hesitation and sensing of unseen body language. It's not as easy as it sounds, particularly if you have a more visual or kinaesthetic preference. You can build this skill by sitting quietly and listening to the world around you, paying acute attention to the tiny noises in the background. Do this often enough and your listening acuity will strengthen.

How will you (continue to) build your virtual coaching muscle to create a great thinking experience for the thinkers with whom you partner?

If it's useful to you, here are some ideas for setting up thinkers for success in the virtual environment, and setting yourself up. This is one way you might introduce these tips.

Suggest that they do the following (and take note yourself too):

➡ Move away from their usual work chair/room so that they can think differently to the way they usually think.

➡ Consider standing or walking for optimum oxygen to the brain – an important prerequisite for creative thinking. The body takes in 11.5 per cent more oxygen when standing compared to sitting (Froboese n.d.).

➡ Join the session from a place that is private, quiet and feels safe to be vulnerable. Do not join:

⇨ from an open office, cafe or thoroughfare in the house, where other people can hear and see every word and move

⇨ from an office with internal glass walls, unless the blinds can be drawn

⇨ while driving – thinking needs undivided attention.

➡ Leave their mobile and any other phones outside the room if it's not being used for the coaching to avoid distraction. Research published by Ward et al. (2017) found that even if mobile phones are turned off, put face down or away, their mere presence reduces people's cognitive capacity.

➡ Turn off all alerts on the computer, to avoid distraction by incoming emails or instant messages.

➡ Take off their self-view so that they aren't distracted.

➡ Schedule 15 minutes in the diary before and after the session, so that they can turn up on time and be fully present, having taken care of biological needs before arriving, rather than hurrying from one meeting to the next without a break.

➡ Keep themselves hydrated for best thinking.

Consider your coaching mindset for virtual coaching and your beliefs about how well it works: any limiting beliefs you hold will limit the quality of your coaching. Also, consider how you can be just as creative in the virtual space as you can face-to-face.

⁂ Shift 66

OLD MINDSET: Rapport is everything
NEW MINDSET: Match for rapport, mismatch for change

Some coaches seem scared to rock the boat. They spend an inordinate amount of time building rapport, not wishing to challenge 'too soon' in case they haven't created enough trust and safety. In fact, most coaches create trust and safety with ease. It seems to come naturally to them – or they have been trained well to match and mirror in a supportive way.

The matching and mirroring of the thinker's tone, pitch, pace, breathing, gestures, energy, words and sensory preferences (auditory, kinaesthetic, visual) fire the mirror neurons in the brain to say 'this person is like me, so they are friend not foe, I can trust them'.

Bandler and Grinder (1989) first developed the technique of matching and mirroring in the 1970s as part of neuro-linguistic programming. The mirroring is immediate, the matching has a slight time lag, but both are meant to be imperceptible to the thinker – although they are perceptible through the mirror neurons. This is known as 'limbic synchrony', which creates rapport. This is goodness.

But as Hawkins and Smith (2013) write, we need to match for rapport and *mismatch* for change. Coaching is all about creating change, small or large. One way to precipitate change is to mismatch after we've built rapport through matching.

Mismatching the thinker's tone, pitch, pace, breathing, gestures, energy, words, sensory preferences and so forth shakes them up. It takes them out of their usual ways of thinking, feeling and sensing. You might ask them to stand up, for example, standing up yourself just as you invite them to do the same. You might quicken the pace of your speaking, or change your energy levels from matching theirs to mismatching them.

But here's the key, according to Hawkins and Smith: you need to model a change that represents the kind of change they are looking to make, emotionally or energetically. If they wish to become more enthusiastic in their influencing of others, you can move to a more enthusiastic way of speaking, using your hands rather than sticking with a match of their quiet, considered tone, pace and still body. This needs to be visible in your body and audible in your tone, not just your words.

In summary, you cannot stay in trust-building forever, or even as long as you think you need to: rapport is important, but challenging the thinker through somatic mismatching is crucial to shifting their thinking and being.

🎭 Shift 67

OLD MINDSET: Tell me more
NEW MINDSET: What meaning do you make of that?

Many coaches have been taught this simple phrase, 'Tell me more' as a way to get a thinker to keep talking. But it's just that – talking – not necessarily new thinking. 'Tell me more' invites storytelling and detail that they already know. It's as though we're asking them to fill us in on the detail, but as we've seen previously, our job as coach is to get them to new thinking, not to go over old ground.

You don't need them to fill you in on all the context if they already know the context themselves. You both may think you need to know the detail to be able to support them, but you don't. Instead, you might replace 'Tell me more' with 'What does that mean to you?', 'What do you make of that?' This takes them deeper, underneath the surface of what they've just said, to the meaning-making. This is a question they won't have been asked by anyone else, so it will get them to new thinking.

Why is meaning-making so important in coaching? Because that's where the 'Aha!' moments lie. Epiphanies don't come from going over the same old ground; neither do they come when we stay at the surface. You need to partner to dig deeper for beliefs, values, importance and significance.

Try questions such as:

➡ 'What is the significance of [a word they have used multiple times]?'
➡ 'What is important to you about that?'
➡ 'Which of your values is this triggering for you?'
➡ 'What is the belief you hold about yourself there?' 'What might be a more useful belief to hold?'
➡ 'When you say X, what feelings does that evoke in you?'

I'm surprised I don't have more to say about this – but why tell you more if you get it already, which I hope you do!

🐾 Shift 68

OLD MINDSET: **I'm curious**
NEW MINDSET: **Get them to be curious**

Another phrase that I hear coming from coaches' mouths is, 'I'm curious' before they ask their question. I suspect this is something they learned from their coach training. Why the lead-in? Is it to soften the question, maybe? To take away the potential sting of a challenging question, or prove that the coach is indeed being curious?

I agree that we should bring a curious mindset. But you don't need to state that you have a curious mindset – you can demonstrate it. Your questions portray that curiosity in and of themselves, as long as they're phrased as open questions without leading to a pre-formulated answer. It feels superfluous then to add 'I'm curious' to the start of a question. Your questions should be as succinct as you can make them without adding fluff.

You're not being curious for your own sake, but for the thinker's, enabling them to get clearer about their thoughts, feelings, needs and desires (see also Shifts 17 and 24). You may need to contract for this at the start of coaching with thinkers who are new to coaching, as they might believe you're looking for a best answer when, in fact, you want to encourage them to find their own answers that are fitting for them.

The mindset that we're taught about being curious is appropriate. The behaviour of preceding our questions with the phrase 'I'm curious' is unnecessary.

♨ Shift 69

OLD MINDSET: Use the established formula
NEW MINDSET: Trust your intuition

When coaches first come out of their coach training, they're often wedded to a model. Following that model (for example, GROW, CLEAR, to name just two) gives them comfort that they are doing it 'right' or the way they 'should' do it. It's understandable – and I remember it well from my own formative years as a coach – that new coaches would want some scaffolding.

It's important to both contract and close well. You've seen that I use mnemonics to guide the beginning and end of my coaching, but even with a model, I notice that not all coaches do these well. Perhaps those are parts of their preferred model to revisit. But as John Whitmore (2012) said of his model, GROW, models can't be (and aren't) the be-all and end-all of our coaching. They're a starting point, within and around which we use our coaching competencies and our own intuition.

Yes, trust the process, but also trust your intuition. Listen to your gut or your sixth sense, whatever you call it.

You can develop your intuition by:

➡ paying attention – to the little voice in your head whispering something to you; your senses, the colours or images you see; physical feelings (like the thinker's headache, for example, or a tightness across the chest); emotions such as sadness or excitement; smells, tastes and touch

➡ listening to your body and all those things it has to offer – you may feel some of the above more strongly than others, so use that to the thinker's advantage

➡ saying aloud what you are noticing – offer what you've sensed to the thinker and ask them what they make of it. Don't interpret it yourself; rather, ask them whether it sheds any light for them. For example: 'I feel tightness in my chest as you say that, and I wonder what that might mean for you?'

There's no model for intuition, but many of us overlook it in favour of rules-based, logical ways of coaching. It's likely that school and work will have knocked the illogical, irrational, non-linear way of being out of you, so you need to build it back up through practice.

Trust yourself. Trust that your intuition plays a part here. You might think that it's your stuff and that it's getting in the way of your paying attention to them; on the contrary, it's usually useful to them.

Trust the thinker, too. They are 'creative, resourceful and whole' after all (Whitworth et al. 1998). They can take or leave your offering, as long as you're prepared to let it go if it doesn't have any meaning for them at this moment in time. They may come back to it as they ponder the session afterwards – or they may not. That's their prerogative.

Finally, trust your presence and that you will find a way to work with the person.

🗒️ Shift 70

OLD MINDSET: I must hold the thinker accountable to progress

NEW MINDSET: I support the thinker to find ways to hold themselves accountable

I hear coaches ask at the beginning of a session: 'What have you achieved since we last met?', or 'What progress have you made towards your goals?'

Indeed, many thinkers want us to check in with them like this, as it is this accountability that moves them towards action in between sessions. But the problem is that it perpetuates a 'Parent–Child' (Berne 1964) relationship rather than a partnership. Just as our teachers asked to see our homework, it creates dependency rather than independence.

Your role as coach is to make yourself redundant, and them independent. You set yourself up for redundancy in every single session by asking them what accountability structures they might like to put in place for themselves back in the workplace that will stand them in good stead for the future, not just for today – to enable them to sustain the changes they wish to make.

At the end of a session, you might ask:

➡ 'What internal and external resources can you draw on to support you in this endeavour?'
➡ 'How will you hold yourself accountable?'

You can then replace the check-in at the start with: 'What is most important for us to work on today?' If the thinker wants to report back, you might ask: 'What have you learned about yourself as a result of the actions you took?', so they can access a deeper self-awareness. If they really want to tell you the whole story of the actions they took, you might encourage them to write those in an email before the session, so you can use the time you have together to get to new thinking rather than going over old ground.

One coach I know worked with a thinker who wanted to report progress by email every day. A coach should not feel duty-bound to reply every day; instead, they could contract for the thinker to write their achievements in a journal instead, enabling them to create a habit that will be sustainable after the coaching is finished.

This is supporting the thinker to find ways to hold themselves accountable.

 # Shift 71

OLD MINDSET: Parrot back what the thinker has told you
NEW MINDSET: Highlight the essence and notice the emotions

We've seen already (in Shift 16) how parroting back takes thinking space away from the thinker. But it seems that coaching schools have taught this as a skill, so we can prove that we've been listening.

'Mmms' and 'yeses', while the thinker is speaking, are another ineffective way of showing that we're listening because they interrupt the thinker's flow. These 'mmms' and 'yeses' can lead the thinker to believe that we want to insert something or that we're chivvying them up.

There are better ways to prove that you are listening, which are more useful to thinkers:

➡ Echo one or two words, or a short phrase.
➡ Ask a question that considers what you've heard. It will be obvious that you've been listening because the question will be based on what they've said or not said, or on their tone or gestures.
➡ Highlight just the essence of what you heard in one short sentence, with an enquiry to follow, for example: 'So you are looking to do X – what are you believing about yourself that is stopping that from happening?'
➡ Notice the emotion in one short sentence, with an enquiry to follow, such as: 'It sounds as though you are really weary. What do you make of that in relation to [what we are working on today]?'

The addition of the enquiry is important to keep the thinking process moving deeper and forward, rather than simply a statement of what you have heard. There is movement here, rather than keeping the thinker in place. This is active listening after all, not passive.

The mindset that you need here isn't to prove that you've been listening; rather, to listen to be useful to the thinking process.

Retrieval practice 6

Stop and take 10 minutes to reflect and retrieve what you've learned from this chapter as a means to solidifying it in your mind and body.

➡ What do you recall from this chapter?
➡ What rings true for you?
➡ What do you see more clearly now?
➡ How does this feel in your body?
➡ What else do you sense?
➡ Which mindsets do you want to discard to make way for more transformational mindsets?
➡ What else did you learn in your coach training that you could discard to be a more masterful coach?

Habit change commitment 6

It's time to commit to trying something different, based on what has resonated with you. This template will help you to make *one* commitment to make *one* small change. When you're comfortable with that, you can make another, and another.

➡ Instead of believing the voice in my head that says...
➡ Which leads me to do/say...
➡ I choose to believe...
➡ And will therefore do/say...
➡ My cue or reminder is...
➡ My immediate reward will be...

You may choose to share this commitment with a coaching buddy for more social accountability.

Now, stop reading and writing: go and experiment with what you have learned, before coming back for more mindset shifts in the rest of the book.

Chapter 7

Mindsets we learned from our coaching experience that we need to discard to be a more masterful coach

As we have practised coaching, we may have built some additional beliefs and mindsets. Some of those will be really useful, and some will not.

Take a moment to think about mindsets you've developed since you completed your coach training, which might be getting in the way of the thinker doing their best thinking.

 # Shift 72

I notice how coaches tend to work in dialogue with their thinkers: a question posed, an answer given, another question asked, another answer given. We sit together, either face-to-face or virtually, and we talk. Your coach training may not have taught you this, but coaches seem to gravitate towards this in their practice.

This presents two obstacles to new thinking:

1. Sitting still can cause thinkers (and coaches) to get stuck. I can't find any research to back this up, but I've seen it in action. The lack of physiological movement can lead to a lack of forward movement in thinking. This is especially true if the thinker is in the same seat that they sit in for their normal work, as that's often where the 'stuckness' was created in the first place.
2. Talking alone does not tap into the thinker's multitude of other intelligences (Gardener 2006[1983]).

We looked at both in Shift 42 about playful experimentation, but let's delve a little deeper here into some of the evidence that movement enhances thinking. First, some research on standing versus sitting: school-aged students who worked at standing desks were 12 per cent more engaged than their seated colleagues (Dornhecker et al. 2015).

Now let's look at walking: according to research by Marily Oppezzo and Daniel Schwartz (2014) at Stanford University, people's creative output increases by an average of 60 per cent when walking. That's an astounding difference and suggests that we should walk every time we coach, not just some of the time!

And what about tapping into other senses, not just talking? Iain McGilchrist (2019) says that there's a risk in this technology-driven, efficiency-focused world that we give too much importance to our conscious, verbal thought, which in itself 'controls the media', convinced that the answers lie in more of its own kind of thinking. Howard Gardener (2006[1983]) wrote that we favour the highly articulate and the logical–mathematical, but that this discounts so many other intelligences. People have many other gifts, and when we neglect these or disregard them, we lose so much richness of wisdom.

The range of intelligences (see Armstrong 2020) includes:

➡ linguistic ('word smart')
➡ logical–mathematical ('number/reasoning smart')
➡ spatial ('picture smart')
➡ bodily–kinaesthetic ('body smart')
➡ musical ('music smart')
➡ interpersonal ('people smart')
➡ intrapersonal ('self-smart')
➡ naturalist ('nature smart').

Leverage these different intelligences in your coaching, not just the first, linguistic intelligence. Some people really struggle to verbalise: in fact, sometimes in coaching, you'll hear them say: 'I don't know how to put this into words.' That's a massive clue for you to partner with and help them to understand the issue using different media. Their other intelligences may have atrophied through lack of use. Some people find it hard to access the bodily–kinaesthetic, or what we now call somatic intelligence, for example. That doesn't mean they can't, just that they are out of practice.

How can you work these other aspects into your coaching, so you're not reliant on just one intelligence that may not be their strong suit in the first place?

👪 Shift 73

OLD MINDSET: Start from the end of the last session

NEW MINDSET: They are now a different person

In their practice, coaches reread their notes from the last session to recall where the thinker got to, and particularly what actions they committed to. As we've already seen, you don't need to remember where the thinker got to at the end of the last session, or what the thinker said they would do next. It's perfectly acceptable to have 'amnesia' as this is their stuff, not yours. They are responsible for remembering (or not) where they got to, and where they have progressed since.

They will have moved on since then anyway. They're a different person as a result of whatever they chose to do (or not do). They've made choices that brought them to this new place. A lot of water has passed under the bridge, as the saying goes.

If you hold on to where they got to last time and ask a question from that vantage point, you will be taking them backwards, not forwards. Hence 'What have you learned about yourself since we last met?', as part of the opening of a new coaching session to move their learning forwards.

✿ Shift 74

OLD MINDSET: Work on the presenting problem

NEW MINDSET: The presenting problem is rarely the problem

No matter how comprehensively the coaching agreement is taught by training schools, I notice that as coaches practise in the real world, they seem to skirt over the coaching agreement to get to the 'real work'.

In discussion with a coach, she said she didn't like pinning people down too much at the beginning of a session because she knew that what came up at the start was not necessarily what needed to be worked on.

She's right – *and* we still need a contract for the presenting problem – because the clearer we get on what it is and is not, the more likely the real problem is to emerge.

If you were to simply run with the first thing that the thinker says they want to talk about, you'd likely be working on something superficial and transactional. Indeed, without questions such as: 'What will be different by the time we finish here today?' and 'How will you know you have got what you need by the end of our X minutes?', you're likely to get lost and meander because you won't have any focus – or you might each understand something different as the focus.

You also need to keep a constant eye out for changes to the contract, as the coaching rarely goes in a straight line:

➡ Where does the thinker's thinking take them?
➡ Do the two of you need to recontract for a new direction?

For example: 'You said at the beginning you wanted to think about X; we seem to now be talking about Y... what path do we need to take from here?' and if they decide to take route Y, ask them the CONTRACTing questions again to establish a new focus.

In addition to checking the pathway that you're taking, you also need to look under the covers. The presenting problem will be suffused with beliefs, assumptions, feelings and values. This may be where the transformational work is hiding in plain sight. You need to listen for tell-tale signals about how *this* thinker thinks, feels, assumes, what they believe and value. Maybe there are some limiting beliefs in there.

I'm currently sharpening my edge around noticing when a thinker is diminishing themselves. It happens more than you might think. If they continue to minimise themselves, the demanding work of change will be even harder as they won't believe in themselves, so this is where the real work is – the work that has to happen before the presenting problem can be resolved.

The mindset here is not to rush to resolve the presenting issue, but to continue to listen for clues that the path is merging onto a different route, and/or that the two of you need to get under the covers.

Meet the thinker where they are, *and* recognise that coaching is not all about productivity or task, which are often the presenting issues.

🌸 Shift 75

OLD MINDSET: Coach the individual
NEW MINDSET: Coach the system

We learn how to coach the individual in our one-to-one coach training, and continue that in our practice (until and unless we also add team or group coaching into our portfolio).

The person in front of us (or to the side in the case of walking coaching) is our focus. They are the centre of the universe in their coaching session. We are thinker-centred. Their goals are paramount; what they want to cover in a session is key; where they want to go is predominant. But they are part of a system, and if we focus purely on the individual without asking about their place in the system and their impact on it, we're missing vital work.

Every life has a story. That life is made up of many constituents: work, home, family, friends, colleagues, etc. Everyone has a ripple effect on those other constituents. That doesn't mean to say that they should be focused on those other people's needs over and above their own, but they do need to figure out where they want to fit in that system, how they want to be, who they want to be – within or maybe outside of that system.

You need to coach the system as much as you coach the individual.

I used to think it was enough to have a contract directly with the thinker. But I have come to see the error of my ways! That one-to-one contract is fine if the thinker is paying for the coaching. But if their company is paying for it, you automatically have an extra client and multiple stakeholders who have expectations about how this person performs in the context of the organisation, its mission and vision.

Hawkins and Turner (2019) describe the one-to-one coaching contract as personal development. That's pretty accurate, I would say, as the thinker decides what they want to work on, and it often has to do with self-leadership.

I think of leadership as multifaceted. There's self-leadership, and we all need to get better at that before we can have a hope of influencing others around us: getting to grips with who we are, what is important to us, how we want to show up in the world, etc. But then there's leadership of others: instantly, you have more stakeholders affected by the coaching – the team members.

Then there's leadership of the organisation, which can only be a collective endeavour – no leader can do this alone, and said leader needs to work with their peers and others to run the business, as well as transform it.

When an organisation commissions you to coach an individual leader, what they really need (although might not be able to name it as such) is systemic coaching, not personal development – so at contracting time, you and the thinker need to identify all of the stakeholders who have a vested interest in this individual stepping up in their world, and to what they want the individual to step up. What will the thinker need to be able to achieve in tomorrow's world to address the needs of those stakeholders?

However, stakeholders go way beyond the organisation. What about societal needs and natural resources, to name but two? What is our responsibility as coach and thinker towards those stakeholders? It might seem overwhelming but none of us is an island; our decisions and actions have a ripple effect on all of these stakeholders.

Coming back to the individual who pays for their own coaching: just because you don't include any other stakeholders in a three-way contract at the start of coaching does not mean there are no stakeholders whose needs are important. Thinkers often bring relationship concerns to coaching, or maybe they want to work out their perspectives and actions around climate change. Both of those, in their own way, are about systems.

Individuals are part of groups (familial or otherwise), which are part of something bigger, which in turn are also part of something bigger. We all live and work in nested systems, one inside another. Figuring out how the thinker wants to act has a ripple effect on those systems, in much the same way as a leader has a ripple effect on the people, teams and functions inside and outside an organisation. Regardless of whether a thinker is paying for their own coaching or not, you need to partner to pay as much attention to the system as you do to the individual.

As well as including questions about stakeholders' needs in your contracting process, you can use constellations to help a thinker see the system more clearly. If I am face-to-face with a thinker, I might pass them a set of buttons or plectrums, and invite them to use these to lay out the constellation in front of them as a map of the system, placing a representative of themselves first then building out from there.

It's a shortcut to seeing more clearly:

➡ who or what is where
➡ how far apart they are
➡ which way they're facing
➡ what shape they are.

There is much richness of learning from this simple activity. If I'm working with them virtually, I might instead ask them to choose objects from their surroundings that represent each of the people or things in the system, and place them in relationship to one another. The objects themselves are often a metaphorical choice, and shed more light still.

This is what we mean by coaching the system. The individual doesn't disappear from this coaching, as they are seeing themselves within the system and their positioning.

✂ Shift 76

OLD MINDSET: Building trust takes time
NEW MINDSET: Cut to the chase

'Don't expect too much, too soon... Build trust gradually...
Trust takes time.'

These are just three of the expressions I found in an Internet search,
which back up the mindset that trust takes time. There may be
occasions when this is true, such as in the sales process. Building
trust with new potential clients can take a number of interactions
over a protracted period of time.

But in coaching, the thinker has chosen to work with you, so there
is trust already. They will have checked out your biography or profile,
and from that decided that you have credible experience – your
authority, as Hawkins and Smith (2013) call it. They will have met you
for a chemistry meeting to check out your presence. And if you've
included some coaching in that chemistry session, they will have
checked out your impact and ability to enable them to shift in some
way – so, they trust you enough to make a decision to work with you.

This means they trust you enough to cut to the chase, so that
they can get value for their investment. What does that mean, 'cut
to the chase'? The saying originated from early silent film, and was
one of film and television producer and director Hal Roach's favourite
expressions to get the story to move along – to the chase. You can
just imagine him saying 'cut that bit out and let's cut to the chase'!

In coaching, 'cut to the chase' means:

➡ getting really clear in each and every session as to what the thinker
wants to walk away with (see also Shift 3 for CONTRACT)
➡ interrupting them to check whether their storytelling is useful
to them, or if they might be better served by focusing on new
thinking (see also Shift 4)
➡ asking them about their assumptions, beliefs and values (see also
Shift 53)

➡ challenging them when they discount themselves (see also Shift 49)
➡ challenging them about their own agency when they fall into victim mode or talk about how others need to change.

In coaching, cutting to the chase does not mean cutting to action. If you go there too soon, you will be missing valuable data that informs better actions or experiments later in the session.

What else do you do to cut to the chase in coaching?

🐍 Shift 77

OLD MINDSET: There are lists of powerful questions

NEW MINDSET: Powerful questions lose their potency in any other coaching conversation

As a beginner coach, how often did you wish for a list of powerful questions in front of you to call on when your head went blank?

Like coaching models, we felt that some questions were inherently better than others, and that we didn't have access to them ourselves. But unless it's a process question (see also Shift 17), a powerful question is only powerful in that one setting, given the person you are working with, their personality, context, stakeholders and a plethora of other aspects that make their situation unique.

A question that works for someone else will rarely work for this thinker because it's not taking their individuality into account. You'll find lists of questions on the Internet, but don't be fooled by them. You will rarely be able to use them because they won't be a good fit.

Trust yourself to come up with a question in the moment that:

➡ draws on what you've heard the thinker say (or not say)
➡ is inspired by the tone of voice you heard or emotions inherent in the way they spoke
➡ makes best use of what you know about the system within which this thinker is working.

What I often notice is that a coach doesn't fail to find a question as much as they ask questions that are for information (to fill the coach in), or are closed, leading or stacked. Practise making your questions open and succinct.

Don't hold on to a question that was brilliant five minutes ago, before the thinker had completed the next five minutes of thinking that took them to a new place. Practise asking questions that are conceived and born in that moment when the thinker has finished thinking, not before. This is where the powerful question comes to life: in the silence. Indeed, they may stumble across their own question, which you can simply play back to them. These are often the questions that they haven't dared to ask themselves before, or not realised they needed to be asked.

Stick with their question rather than moving on to your own question. And don't worry if the syntax isn't quite right: it will land – or it won't. If it doesn't, you can clarify, but don't clarify straightaway, making a stacked question, as that first question will likely be more powerful if asked as is.

🧘 Shift 78

OLD MINDSET: Build psychometric tests, 360-degree feedback or personality assessments into the start of a coaching programme

NEW MINDSET: Assessments set up a Parent–Child rather than an Adult–Adult relationship

I know a good many coaches who insert some kind of assessment into the start of their coaching programme. Some organisations and associate companies require that coaches are certified to do this. Assessments can be useful to a person who wishes to understand themselves better, to get a picture of their strengths and stretches. For example, per Luft and Ingham's (1961) Johari Window, with a good debrief 360s can:

➡ show up aspects that are known to others, but not known to the thinker

➡ reconfirm qualities and limitations that are known to others and known to self

➡ identify attributes that are known to the thinker, but hidden from others.

With this data, the thinker can decide where to focus their coaching goals. That's all goodness.

When asked whether I start a coaching programme with an assessment of some kind, I say 'no'. I go on to explain that the difficulty with me doing that, then moving into coaching, is that it sets up a 'Parent–Child' (Berne 1964) relationship – which is far from the 'Adult–Adult' relationship we aspire to in coaching.

Why 'Parent–Child'? Because the person who debriefs the instrument has expertise in interpreting the tool, and this expertise gives them more power than the thinker, who is less expert.

The debriefer has an advantage over the thinker because they understand the significance of the highs and lows of the report, and the connections between the various parts. The thinker starts the relationship in a 'less than' position, no matter how hard the debriefer tries to be a partner in the interpretation of the results, or invites them to think for themselves about the meaning of the results.

This is why the ICF doesn't accept time debriefing an instrument in coaches' experience logs. Debriefing an instrument is seen as feedback, not coaching.

In my experience, it's better to have two different people collaborating with the thinker if an instrument is required. The debriefer would work with the thinker to help them interpret the results. The thinker then decides how much or little of the results to share with their coach, and can use the results to inform the shape of their coaching programme. The power is now with the thinker to share or not. You may think this risks the thinker not sharing things they're ashamed of, or neglecting feedback that doesn't suit their own self-view. But this is their coaching, and they get to drive the agenda. As you build the partnership together and as trust increases, they will likely open up more about this feedback that they chose at the start to keep private. That's their prerogative.

If you do wish to offer assessments as part of your coaching programme, I suggest you tag-team with another person who can debrief the instrument and then pass over to you.

🎁 Shift 79

OLD MINDSET: When a session is over, it's over

NEW MINDSET: Closing the session fully allows for continued new thinking afterwards

I see so many coaches end their sessions abruptly: it's as though they want to get as much accomplished in the time they have with a thinker, that they forget to keep an eye on the time. Even as they approach five minutes before the end, they're still asking divergent questions rather than convergent; questions that open up the thinking rather than ones that bring the session to a close.

Good endings are vital to ensure that thinking and forward motion continues post-session. I suspect there are many (conscious or unconscious) beliefs that contribute to abrupt endings:

➡ We must cover everything we set out to cover.
➡ 'I've started, so I'll finish.' (the famous catchphrase of Magnus Magnusson, the first presenter of TV quiz *Mastermind*)
➡ I add value by getting the thinker to a resolution to their issue.
➡ They can't do the thinking on their own outside of the session.

If you were to replace these mindsets with the following, you could give the ending the attention it needs:

➡ Any progress is good progress. (Amabile and Kramer 2011)
➡ We get to wherever we get to in the time we have together.
➡ The thinker is 'creative, resourceful and whole' (Whitworth et al. 1998) and can continue thinking and moving forward without me, if we plan for that.
➡ Good endings make way for great new beginnings. (Bridges 2004).

With these different beliefs in mind, you can shift your behaviour away from a bumpy landing into a much smoother transition from coaching back into day-to-day life.

Good endings in coaching might look something like this CLOSE (which we already discussed in depth in Shift 17):

Consolidation: 'We have X minutes left. You said you wanted X today... what progress have you made towards that?' 'What experiments are you committing to after the session that will continue your progress?'
Learning: 'What are you hoping to learn from your experiments?' 'What have you learned about yourself today that you can apply in this situation and beyond?'
Obstacles: 'What might get in your way?'
Support: 'How will you hold yourself accountable?' 'What support mechanisms might you put in place?' 'What internal and external resources can you draw on?'
End: 'On that note, is that enough for today?'

As you can see, this calls on the thinker to pull together the threads of what they've been thinking about, and make some commitments to themselves post-session. This gives them the momentum to keep going after the session is over, and makes room for a great new beginning to the next chapter of their growth. Each session creates an outline for the next chapter; then the next chapter in between sessions is given life through new ways of being.

And if they haven't finished everything they set out to achieve in the session? Don't tell them to bring it next time, as that presupposes they can't make progress alone. Instead, ask a question about where they will get the support to figure that out.

🕊️ Shift 80

As we've seen previously, some coaches follow a model of 90–120 minutes of coaching, while others stick with 60 minutes. Still others go for shorter 30–45-minute sessions. Those who learned to work with 90 minutes at the start of their coaching practice find it hard to adapt to shorter sessions and vice-versa. I started my coaching career coaching for 60 minutes at a time, and when asked to coach for 120 minutes, I couldn't imagine how to make it last that long!

We do need to contract for a length of time per session, so that we can both have clear diaries for that duration, plus some additional time before and after to get prepared and reflect. But here's the thing: sometimes the thinker has finished before you've used up all that time. They've done some great thinking, made a breakthrough and are ready to get on with the actual work of doing and being different. They don't need to keep going, just so that you can say you used all the time you had together.

How do you know that they are done? Ask them. For example:

➡ 'You said at the beginning that you wanted X; where are you with that now?'
➡ 'Your question today was X; how are we doing in finding an answer to that?'

Then let them know how much time you still have left, and ask how they would like to use it: 'What would be useful in our remaining 20 minutes together?'

If they are done, and if you've built a good partnership where they feel they can say they're done, they will tell you at this point that they're ready to wrap up – so, move to CLOSE. Don't just stop dead, but end the session well (see also Shifts 17 and 79).

On several occasions over the course of my coaching career, a thinker has decided to work alone for the rest of their time on the action they've decided to take, as they want to strike while the iron is hot. For example, writing a business case while ideas are fresh in their mind, drafting an email requesting a meeting, picking up the phone to have a conversation or creating a spreadsheet to address one of their concerns.

This is their choice to use the time in this way, and they are continuing to get value from the time that they have set aside in their diary for the coaching. They don't need you there to be able to do this, but the time is a gift to them to get it done before they slot back into their busy operations.

The new mindset is that you are done when you are done! Again, move to CLOSE at this point rather than carrying on just because you are contracted to work for longer. You will over-egg the pudding if you take control of the agenda and keep going.

This can apply equally to the number of sessions you plan for. If a thinker feels that they have enough from one session rather than the contracted four, they are done. No need to continue just because that's what has been paid for (although you may wish to think about how you structure your contracts with organisational stakeholders: for example, are you charging for a set number of sessions or hours, or completion of objectives?).

In fact, maybe it's time to look at how many sessions you do contract for, and whether each thinker really does need that many. Single-session coaching might be all they need to make a break-through – and you both need to believe that this is possible. If you think it will take six sessions, often it will. The work expands (or contracts) to the time you have available (you will recognise this as Parkinson's Law; Parkinson 1955).

🛕 Shift 81

'We don't have time... I don't have what it takes... We are in competition.'

Why do we see resources such as time, skills, courage and customers as scarce? I get that our planetary resources *are* scarce, and that time and personal energy are finite. But much of the time in coaching, we hear this scarcity mentality applied to all sorts of areas of life that don't need to be treated as finite.

It takes artful questions to move thinkers towards an abundance mentality – and it takes role-modelling from you. If you talk about time as a scarce commodity in the session (e.g. 'we *only* have five minutes left') instead of as an abundance of possibility (e.g. 'we have a full five minutes left'), you'll be encouraging the thinker to live with the same paradigm. If you insert time into your first sentence, the thinker may also see it as a scarce commodity, for example:

'In our 45 minutes together today, what would you like to cover?'

Compare this with:

'What would be most useful for you to think about today? [Give space for them to answer.] And in our 45 minutes, which piece of that would be most useful?'

You see how the first may limit the big-picture goal before the session has even begun, whereas the second allows for the big picture, then a funnel from that to what would be most useful in the time.

If you restrict what you can and can't do because you're working virtually, you're doing the same: demonstrating limiting beliefs in the way you conduct your work (see also Shift 65). And if you see other coaches as competition, you're demonstrating a belief that there's a limit on the amount of work to go around.

Not only is the thinker 'creative, resourceful and whole' (Whitworth et al. 1998), but also your time together: the resources you have available to you are more abundant than you might first think; the people in your network are bountiful. This is a mindset shift that you can embody as a way of inviting the thinker to do the same.

🖼️ Shift 82

OLD MINDSET: Keep calm and carry on
NEW MINDSET: Take recovery time *before* **you need it**

The expression 'Keep Calm and Carry On' has become somewhat of a meme in modern society, but it originated in 1939 before the Second World War, to motivate the British population to do just that in the face of war. Another expression that we Brits know well is around keeping a stiff upper lip. No trembling of the lip in fear or other emotion!

The problem is this encourages unhelpful behaviour, struggling on even when we really need to take a break and re-resource ourselves. Those people with a 'Be Strong' driver (Kahler 1975; see also Shift 27) are particularly affected by this: putting a brave face on things and pushing on through, even when they are exhausted.

This is bad for your own mental health, and bad for thinkers, as they won't get the best from you – even if you think you can disguise your distress. You may not even recognise your own distress, so you may not be consciously disguising it.

ICF Competency 2, 'Embodies a Coaching Mindset'. includes reference to how we regulate our emotions in the coaching space, while still being authentic.

➡ What are your personal signs of distress?
➡ The early warning signs?
➡ How do you know that you need to take recovery time before you fall over?

As we've identified previously, each of us has a uniquely sized 'stress container' (Mental Health First Aid England n.d.) – and we shouldn't compare the size of our container with someone else's. People often compare their own load with that of others, saying they don't have anywhere near as much to worry about as them; but given that our stress container may be smaller than others', we shouldn't be comparing with theirs, only with our normal levels of stress.

Is your personal container brimming over with too much stress? What's causing it, and what can you do to relieve it?

If you also imagine that the container has a tap which can be opened to let out some of the stress, it's worth thinking about what you need to do that. (For me, it's running, yoga, painting, getting out in nature, talking to a friend, escaping into a good book, a bunch of flowers – I could go on. If I allow work and stress to get in the way of these, my stress container will overflow.)

Please notice the early signs that your container is filling to the brim, so you can open the tap before you really need to: eustress (just enough positive stress) is good; distress is not. Eustress keeps you on your toes. Distress makes you fall over.

Thinkers need you to be in eustress: not only because that's where you can do your best coaching, but also because it's good role-modelling and can support them to reduce their own distress in favour of eustress.

 # Shift 83

OLD MINDSET: Pride comes before a fall

NEW MINDSET: Account for your whole self, and enable thinkers to account for their whole self

Oh, how I hate this expression, 'pride comes before a fall'. There have been times in my life when I've been really proud of myself and how I've shown up – not to mention pride in what I've achieved.

But I so frequently get the little voice in my head, saying: 'Be careful! Don't get too big for your boots, don't shout about it, it'll all be taken away any minute now if you make too big a thing of it' (see also Shift 12). Shut up voice, please!

I retreat into my little girl whenever I think in this way. I make myself smaller than I really am. I retract and reduce. This is not the voice I want to be listening to if I want to be my best, bravest, boldest or biggest.

This mindset shift is just as much about who you are alone, as who you are with a thinker.

Why do we have such joy-sapping expressions anyway? Google's English dictionary defines the expression as 'if you're too conceited or self-important, something will happen to make you look foolish.' OK, now that is different. Being conceited is not the same as being proud; neither does pride take away from anyone else's importance. We can all be proud of who we are and what we have accomplished, without detracting from others' pride in themselves.

This is not a competition; there's an abundance of goodness that we can all bring into the world.

The thing is, if we show up with beliefs such as this, we can bet that thinkers will too. Our job is to help ourselves first to account for our whole self: notice and accept, rather than judge ourselves. This word 'accounting' is the opposite of discounting. In Transactional Analysis terms, and according to Schiff et al. (1975), discounting is 'an internal mechanism which involves people minimising or ignoring some aspect of themselves, others or the reality [of the] situation'. Accounting is the opposite: taking into account aspects of yourself, others or the reality of a situation. You can account for yourself by knowing who you are, your strengths and stretches, what you have achieved in life – everything that makes you the unique human being that you are.

Do the work on yourself first. None of us coaches are perfect; we're all works in progress. But we do need to continue to address these voices from our past that get in our own way, so that we can legitimately support others to do the same. This feels like a great message to end on!

Retrieval practice 7

This is your final retrieval practice. Stop for just a few minutes to reflect on what you've read and can recall, all in service of retaining the learning.

Here are some questions for you to write the answers to. Please don't skip over them – they will really help you to assimilate what you have read:

➡ What do you recall from this chapter about coaching practice?
➡ What rings true to you?
➡ What do you see more clearly now?
➡ How does this feel in your body?
➡ What else do you sense?
➡ Which mindsets do you want to discard to make way for more transformational mindsets?
➡ What else has your coaching experience instilled in you that you could discard to be a more masterful coach?

Habit change commitment 7

It's time to commit to trying something different, based on what has resonated with you. This template will help you to make *one* commitment to make *one* small change. When you're comfortable with that, you can make another, and another.

➡ Instead of believing the voice in my head that says...
➡ Which leads me to do/say...
➡ I choose to believe...
➡ And will therefore do/say...
➡ My cue or reminder is...
➡ My immediate reward will be...

You may choose to share this commitment with a coaching buddy for more social accountability.

Now, stop reading and writing: go and experiment with what you have learned, before coming back to complete the rest of the book.

Summary

Eighty-three mindset shifts. That's a lot – and there are probably many more. You won't need to work on all of them, as you will already have shifted many over the course of your coaching experience.

Which are the ones that you wish to personally pay attention to, as you enter into each coaching session? Don't bite off more than you can chew. Take a couple at a time, get unconsciously competent with those, as Broadwell (1969) described it, then add another couple. However, don't get complacent in that unconscious competence space, as that is where you will get lazy and cut corners.

I was running a training session with a group of health workers who coach on the side of their role, and they realised that they still need many of the old mindsets to do their jobs well. But if they move straight from their job into the coaching space, the danger is taking those same mindsets into the coaching room, to the detriment of the thinker's thinking.

Please do take time out in between your non-thinker-facing work and coaching work to shift into the more useful mindsets for coaching. It will take some conscious effort and a little bit of time to offload the less than useful and embrace the more useful mindsets.

Here are the main messages worth reiterating as you come to the end of this book:

➡ Coaching is a joint endeavour, so everything that we believe, do and say should reflect that.
➡ The purpose is to get to new thinking, not go over old ground, and each mindset shift reflects this.
➡ New thinking leads to transformational change, now or in the long run. Pushing too hard, too fast creates short-term wins but long-term falling-back to old ways. Aim for transformation by

asking questions that take the thinking vertically deeper rather than horizontally forwards.

➡ Like a personal trainer, your job is not to do the heavy lifting. The trainee lifts the weights themselves to build their own body muscles. The thinker does the hard thinking in order to build their thinking muscles.

Afterword

At the start of this book, I planted the seed that you might invest in mentor-coaching, so that you can get some high-quality feedback on your coaching. Remember, 'Mentor coaching is for life, not just credentialling' (Norman 2020). Mentor-coaching is also a shortcut to becoming an advanced coach.

Just because I've written this book doesn't mean that I'm the perfect coach. There's no such thing. I am a work-in-progress, just like you. As I put my own coaching under the spotlight in my own mentor-coaching, I see, hear and notice what I didn't before – and in doing so, I bring more supercharge to coaching each and every time I coach. I find this thrilling, knowing that I'm resharpening my edge over and over again for the benefit of the thinkers with whom I work.

I hope you will have been trying out some of the ideas we've worked through in the book, and now it might be time to shine a light on those 'blind spots' that you can't see, hear or notice alone. You might be using words that aren't as useful as they could be to each thinker, but haven't picked up on them for yourself yet; or missing opportunities to challenge; or something else entirely.

Your first step is to make recordings of your coaching and listen back to those. Here are some ideas for enhancing the learning from listening to your recordings (I have used the ICF competencies here, but you could substitute your own coaching body's competencies).

1. Create a transcript (using Otter.ai or other similar software), and listen to the recording with the transcript in front of you.
2. Listen first to yourself, and use the PCC Markers (see Appendix 2) or equivalent to mark on your transcript which ones you demonstrate every time you speak or stay silent (e.g. PCC Markers 3.1, 5.2, 7.3).

3. Also mark where you see opportunities to insert a question or observation that would demonstrate more of the Markers.

4. Look for patterns, for example:

⇨ How thorough is your coaching agreement? (See PCC Markers 3.1–3.4.)

⇨ How accordion-like is the coaching agreement, ebbing and flowing rather than rushing through?

⇨ How much do you use partnering language? (See PCC Markers 3.1–3.2, 3.4, 4.4, 5.3, 8.5–8.9.)

⇨ How invitational are you versus directive? ('Embodies a coaching mindset') Do you slip into mentoring or consulting at any time?

⇨ How many closed questions do you use? (See PCC Marker 7.6.)

⇨ How many times do you stack questions? (See PCC Marker 7.6.)

⇨ What percentage of time do you speak in comparison with them? (See PCC Markers 6.7, 7.8.)

⇨ Do you interrupt their new thinking? (See PCC Marker 6.6; it's OK to interrupt their story, with permission, if it's known thinking.)

⇨ How often do you coach the problem rather than the person? (See PCC Markers 5.1, 7.2, 8.2.)

⇨ At what point in the coaching do you start asking action-oriented questions?

⇨ Have you explored enough to allow for transformative action rather than transactional?

⇨ How thorough are you with the ending? (See PCC Markers 8.1–8.9.)

5. In your second pass, listen to the thinker to see what you missed:

⇨ What do you notice in their words or expressions that you could have reflected back and explored with them? (See PCC Markers 6.2–6.5, 7.5, 8.8.)

⇨ How challenging are you?

⇨ What opportunities could you see for more challenge?

6. Overall, what are you proudest of in the way you coached in this recording? Which competencies did you demonstrate the most?
7. Overall, what would you like to do differently in your practice? What did you learn from the PCC Markers about how to do that?
8. What questions do you have for your mentor-coach? Which parts of the recording would you most like to listen to with your mentor-coach to get their feedback? (Note the timestamps to make it easy to fast-forward.)

Once you have wrung out the learning you can get from listening alone to your recordings, I highly recommend commissioning a mentor-coach.

Mentor-coaching is 'observed coaching with feedback against a set of competencies, which sharpens the coach's all-round presence' (Norman 2018). You can read much more about mentor-coaching in my book *Mentor Coaching: A Practical Guide* (2020). But reading isn't the same as finding someone to work with!

Where do you find a mentor-coach?

Well, you have been on a journey with this mentor-coach, so perhaps you might reach out to me at clare@clarenormancoachingassociates.com. I also work alongside associate mentor-coaches, whom I have trained and can highly recommend. Other mentor-coaches are available, and you can search for ICF-aligned ones in the mentor-coaching registry on the ICF website: https://coachingfederation.org/find-a-coach. If you're a member of a different coaching body, you may wish to ask your supervisor for this kind of support.

Keep resharpening that edge. Although it may feel vulnerable to put yourself under the scrutiny of another coach to give you feedback, it is well worth the discomfort. Alongside supervision, mentor-coaching is the most individualised, highest-impact development I have ever invested in for my own growth as a coach.

Acknowledgements

This book would not have been written had it not been for the coaches with whom I've worked who invited me to observe them and give feedback on their coaching. They were brave enough to put themselves and their coaching mindsets and skillsets under the microscope. To them, I say thank you for giving me the raw material for the book, and congratulations on continually sharpening your coaching edge.

Thank you to my own mentor-coaches and supervisors over the years, for enabling me to sharpen my own edge: Eunice Aquilina, Danielle Brooks, Bernadette Cass, Diane Clutterbuck, Duncan Coppack, Sue Gravells, Michelle Lucas, Tara Nolan, Claire Pedrick, Anne Powell, Eve Turner and the late Angela Wagner.

Then there are all of the coaches I interviewed to make sure I wasn't the only one who experienced the script formations that I discuss here in the book. I tried to get some variety across cultures, but I realise there are many cultures not represented here. Nonetheless, I was surprised at how similar our experiences were: Joe Baker, Jaya Bhateja, William Buist, Bernadette Cass, Diane Clutterbuck, Yvonne Egbuna, Sue Gammons, Annabel Graham, Sue Gravells, Alison Hughes-Lewis, Sheela Hobden, Satya Kumar, Gamal Lewis, Michelle Lucas, Barry McGrath, Anand Manickaraj, Jeannette Marshall, Jason Miller, Ishha Nagrath, Simon North, Seshandrinathan Prakash, Netysha Santos, Marie Smith, Dave Stitt, Lanre Sulola and Andrew Wood. Thank you all for your time and thoughts.

Thank you to those coaches who partnered with me to create my definition of coaching (I'm sorry to say that I have lost track of who you all are, but I know you'll know yourselves), and to Paul Tanenbaum for his challenge that led to an update to the definition.

Thank you to Yvette Elcock for her stimulating and provocative insights, which led to the Shift on difference.

Thank you to my book buddy group, led by Sue Richardson. Within the first month of our work together you had motivated me to finish the first draft when I had previously stalled. As we continued to work together, your support and challenge were invaluable to me.

Thank you to everyone at The Right Book Company for making this book the best it could be. I really appreciate all your feedback and encouragement along the way to publication.

Thank you, Lucy Day, for your fabulous questions and suggestions when you read my first draft. Your feedback really made a difference to the final book.

Thank you, Bob Gerard, for your careful editing and your continued presence in my life. Please know that when I wrote about the way managers show up, that wasn't describing you! Thank you, Jonathan Passmore and Bob Gerard for your personalised forewords.

Thank you to Mark for giving me space to write, and for cooking me sustaining food while I did so!

Finally, thank you to all the thought leaders in coaching who have come before, and all who will come in the future, for shaping our profession and making it such a masterful tribe.

Appendix 1
ICF Competencies, current in 2022

Reprinted with kind permission of the International Coaching Federation.

A. Foundation

1. Demonstrates ethical practice

Definition: Understands and consistently applies coaching ethics and standards of coaching.

1. Demonstrates personal integrity and honesty in interactions with clients, sponsors and relevant stakeholders.
2. Is sensitive to clients' identity, environment, experiences, values and beliefs.
3. Uses language appropriate and respectful to clients, sponsors and relevant stakeholders.
4. Abides by the ICF Code of Ethics and upholds the Core Values.
5. Maintains confidentiality with client information per stakeholder agreements and pertinent laws.
6. Maintains the distinctions between coaching, consulting, psychotherapy and other support professions.
7. Refers clients to other support professionals, as appropriate.

2. Embodies a coaching mindset

Definition: Develops and maintains a mindset that is open, curious, flexible and client-centred.

1. Acknowledges that clients are responsible for their own choices.
2. Engages in ongoing learning and development as a coach.
3. Develops an ongoing reflective practice to enhance one's coaching.
4. Remains aware of and open to the influence of context and culture on self and others.
5. Uses awareness of self and one's intuition to benefit clients.
6. Develops and maintains the ability to regulate one's emotions.
7. Mentally and emotionally prepares for sessions.
8. Seeks help from outside sources when necessary.

B. Co-Creating the relationship

3. Establishes and maintains agreements

Definition: Partners with the client and relevant stakeholders to create clear agreements about the coaching relationship, process, plans and goals. Establishes agreements for the overall coaching engagement as well as those for each coaching session.

1. Explains what coaching is and is not and describes the process to the client and relevant stakeholders.
2. Reaches agreement about what is and is not appropriate in the relationship, what is and is not being offered, and the responsibilities of the client and relevant stakeholders.
3. Reaches agreement about the guidelines and specific parameters of the coaching relationship such as logistics, fees, scheduling, duration, termination, confidentiality and inclusion of others.
4. Partners with the client and relevant stakeholders to establish an overall coaching plan and goals.
5. Partners with the client to determine client–coach compatibility.
6. Partners with the client to identify or reconfirm what they want to accomplish in the session.
7. Partners with the client to define what the client believes they need to address or resolve to achieve what they want to accomplish in the session.

8. Partners with the client to define or reconfirm measures of success for what the client wants to accomplish in the coaching engagement or individual session.
9. Partners with the client to manage the time and focus of the session.
10. Continues coaching in the direction of the client's desired outcome unless the client indicates otherwise.
11. Partners with the client to end the coaching relationship in a way that honours the experience.

4. Cultivates trust and safety

Definition: Partners with the client to create a safe, supportive environment that allows the client to share freely. Maintains a relationship of mutual respect and trust.

1. Seeks to understand the client within their context which may include their identity, environment, experiences, values and beliefs.
2. Demonstrates respect for the client's identity, perceptions, style and language and adapts one's coaching to the client.
3. Acknowledges and respects the client's unique talents, insights and work in the coaching process.
4. Shows support, empathy and concern for the client.
5. Acknowledges and supports the client's expression of feelings, perceptions, concerns, beliefs and suggestions.
6. Demonstrates openness and transparency as a way to display vulnerability and build trust with the client.

5. Maintains presence

Definition: Is fully conscious and present with the client, employing a style that is open, flexible, grounded and confident.

1. Remains focused, observant, empathetic and responsive to the client.
2. Demonstrates curiosity during the coaching process.
3. Manages one's emotions to stay present with the client.
4. Demonstrates confidence in working with strong client emotions during the coaching process.
5. Is comfortable working in a space of not knowing.
6. Creates or allows space for silence, pause or reflection.

C. Communicating effectively

6. Listens actively

Definition: Focuses on what the client is and is not saying to fully understand what is being communicated in the context of the client systems and to support client self-expression.

1. Considers the client's context, identity, environment, experiences, values and beliefs to enhance understanding of what the client is communicating.
2. Reflects or summarises what the client communicated to ensure clarity and understanding.
3. Recognises and enquires when there is more to what the client is communicating.
4. Notices, acknowledges and explores the client's emotions, energy shifts, non-verbal cues or other behaviours.
5. Integrates the client's words, tone of voice and body language to determine the full meaning of what is being communicated.
6. Notices trends in the client's behaviours and emotions across sessions to discern themes and patterns.

7. Evokes awareness

Definition: Facilitates client insight and learning by using tools and techniques such as powerful questioning, silence, metaphor or analogy.

1. Considers client experience when deciding what might be most useful.
2. Challenges the client as a way to evoke awareness or insight.
3. Asks questions about the client, such as their way of thinking, values, needs, wants and beliefs.
4. Asks questions that help the client explore beyond current thinking.
5. Invites the client to share more about their experience in the moment.
6. Notices what is working to enhance client progress.
7. Adjusts the coaching approach in response to the client's needs.

8. Helps the client identify factors that influence current and future patterns of behaviour, thinking or emotion.
9. Invites the client to generate ideas about how they can move forward and what they are willing or able to do.
10. Supports the client in reframing perspectives.
11. Shares observations, insights and feelings, without attachment, that have the potential to create new learning for the client.

D. Cultivating learning and growth

8. Facilitates client growth

Definition: Partners with the client to transform learning and insight into action. Promotes client autonomy in the coaching process.

1. Works with the client to integrate new awareness, insight or learning into their worldview and behaviours.
2. Partners with the client to design goals, actions and accountability measures that integrate and expand new learning.
3. Acknowledges and supports client autonomy in the design of goals, actions and methods of accountability.
4. Supports the client in identifying potential results or learning from identified action steps.
5. Invites the client to consider how to move forward, including resources, support and potential barriers.
6. Partners with the client to summarise learning and insight within or between sessions.
7. Celebrates the client's progress and successes.
8. Partners with the client to close the session.

Appendix 2

Professional Certified Coach Markers, current in 2022

Reprinted with kind permission of the International Coaching Federation.

Assessment Markers are the indicators that an assessor is trained to listen for to determine which ICF Core Competencies are evident in a recorded coaching conversation and to what extent. The Markers are behaviours that represent demonstration of the Core Competencies in a coaching conversation at the Professional Certified Coach (PCC) level.

These Markers support a performance evaluation process that is fair, consistent, valid, reliable, repeatable and defensible.

The PCC Markers may also support coaches, coach trainers and mentor-coaches in identifying areas for growth and skill development in coaching at the PCC level; however, they should always be used in the context of Core Competency development. The PCC Markers should not be used as a checklist in a formulaic manner for passing the PCC performance evaluation (ICF 2019).

Competency 1: Demonstrates ethical practice

Familiarity with the ICF Code of Ethics and its application is required for all levels of coaching. Successful PCC candidates will demonstrate coaching that is aligned with the ICF Code of Ethics and will remain consistent in the role of a coach.

Competency 2:
Embodies a coaching mindset

Embodying a coaching mindset – a mindset that is open, curious, flexible and client-centred – is a process that requires ongoing learning and development, establishing a reflective practice and preparing for sessions. These elements take place over the course of a coach's professional journey and cannot be fully captured in a single moment in time. However, certain elements of this competency may be demonstrated within a coaching conversation. These particular behaviours are articulated and assessed through the following PCC Markers: 4.1, 4.3–4.4, 5.1–5.4, 6.1, 6.5, 7.1 and 7.5.

Competency 3:
Establishes and maintains agreements

3.1: Coach partners with the client to identify or reconfirm what the client wants to accomplish in this session.

3.2: Coach partners with the client to define or reconfirm measure(s) of success for what the client wants to accomplish in this session.

3.3: Coach enquires about or explores what is important or meaningful to the client about what they want to accomplish in this session.

3.4: Coach partners with the client to define what the client believes they need to address to achieve what they want to accomplish in this session.

Competency 4:
Cultivates trust and safety

4.1: Coach acknowledges and respects the client's unique talents, insights and work in the coaching process.

4.2: Coach shows support, empathy or concern for the client.

4.3: Coach acknowledges and supports the client's expression of feelings, perceptions, concerns, beliefs or suggestions.

4.4: Coach partners with the client by inviting the client to respond in any way to the coach's contributions and accepts the client's response.

Competency 5:
Maintains presence

5.1: Coach acts in response to the whole person of the client (the who).

5.2: Coach acts in response to what the client wants to accomplish throughout this session (the what).

5.3: Coach partners with the client by supporting the client to choose what happens in this session.

5.4: Coach demonstrates curiosity to learn more about the client.

5.5: Coach allows for silence, pause or reflection.

Competency 6:
Listens actively

6.1: Coach's questions and observations are customised by using what the coach has learned about who the client is or the client's situation.

6.2: Coach enquires about or explores the words the client uses.

6.3: Coach enquires about or explores the client's emotions.

6.4: Coach explores the client's energy shifts, non-verbal cues or other behaviours.

6.5: Coach enquires about or explores how the client currently perceives themself or their world.

6.6: Coach allows the client to complete speaking without interrupting unless there is a stated coaching purpose to do so.

6.7: Coach succinctly reflects or summarises what the client communicated to ensure the client's clarity and understanding.

Competency 7:
Evokes awareness

7.1: Coach asks questions about the client, such as their current way of thinking, feeling, values, needs, wants, beliefs or behaviour.

7.2: Coach asks questions to help the client explore beyond the client's current thinking or feeling to new or expanded ways of thinking or feeling about themself (the who).

7.3: Coach asks questions to help the client explore beyond the client's current thinking or feeling to new or expanded ways of thinking or feeling about their situation (the what).

7.4: Coach asks questions to help the client explore beyond current thinking, feeling or behaving toward the outcome the client desires.

7.5: Coach shares – with no attachment – observations, intuitions, comments, thoughts or feelings, and invites the client's exploration through verbal or tonal invitation.

7.6: Coach asks clear, direct, primarily open-ended questions, one at a time, at a pace that allows for thinking, feeling or reflection by the client.

7.7: Coach uses language that is generally clear and concise.

7.8: Coach allows the client to do most of the talking.

Competency 8:
Facilitates client growth

8.1: Coach invites or allows the client to explore progress toward what the client wanted to accomplish in this session.

8.2: Coach invites the client to state or explore the client's learning in this session about themself (the who).

8.3: Coach invites the client to state or explore the client's learning in this session about their situation (the what).

8.4: Coach invites the client to consider how they will use new learning from this coaching session.

8.5: Coach partners with the client to design post-session thinking, reflection or action.

8.6: Coach partners with the client to consider how to move forward, including resources, support or potential barriers.

8.7: Coach partners with the client to design the best methods of accountability for themself.

8.8: Coach celebrates the client's progress and learning.

8.9: Coach partners with the client on how they want to complete this session.

Bibliography

Introduction

The Empire Strikes Back (1980) Dir. I. Kershner, LucasFilm.

Whitworth, L., Kimsey-House, H. and Sandahl, P. (1998) *Co-active Coaching*, Palo Alto, CA: Davies Black Publishing.

Covey, S. (1999) *The 7 Habits of Highly Effective People*, New York: Simon & Schuster.

Stewart, I. and Joines, V. (1987) *TA Today: A New Introduction to Transactional Analysis*, Kiddington: Centre Press.

Wilkinson, D. (2018) *The Oxford Review Research-based Guide to Unlearning*, Nottingham: Russell Press Limited.

Kline, N. (2002) *Time to Think*, London: Cassell.

Norman, C.E. (2020) *Mentor Coaching: A Practical Guide*, Maidenhead: Open University Press.

International Coaching Federation (ICF) (2022) Mentor coaching. Available at: https://coachfederation.org/mentor-coaching, accessed: 30/3/2022.

Norman, C.E. (2018) Locked-in learning, *Coaching at Work* 13(6): 42–45.

Eckstein, R. (1969) Concerning the teaching and learning of psychoanalysis, *Journal of the American Psychoanalytic Association* 17(2): 312–332.

International Coaching Federation (ICF) (2019) Core competencies. Available at: https://coachfederation.org/core-competencies, accessed: 30/3/2022.

ICF (2020) PCC Markers. Available at: https://coachingfederation.org/pcc-markers, accessed: 24/3/2022.

Norman, C.E. (2020) *Mentor Coaching: A Practical Guide*, Maidenhead: Open University Press.

Brown, P.C., Roediger III, H.L. and McDaniel, M.A. (2014) *Make it Stick: The Science of Successful Learning*, Cambridge, MA: Belknap Press.

How to use this book for continuous professional development

Dweck, C. (2017) *Mindset: Changing the Way You Think to Fulfil Your Potential*, 6th edition, London: Robinson.

Agarwal, P.K. and Bain, P.M. (2019) *The Power of Teaching: Unleash the Science of Learning*, Hoboken, NJ: Wiley Publishing.

Brown, P.C., Roediger, H.L., III and McDaniel, M.A. (2014) *Make it Stick: The Science of Successful Learning*, Cambridge, MA: Belknap Press.

Clear, J. (2018) *Atomic Habits*, New York: Random House Business.

Heffernan, M. (2020) *Uncharted: How to Map the Future Together*, New York: Simon & Schuster.

Eckstein, R. (1969) Concerning the teaching and learning of psycho-analysis, *Journal of the American Psychoanalytic Association* 17(2): 312–332.

Chapter 1

Edmondson, A. (1999) Psychological safety and learning behaviour in work teams, *Administrative Science Quarterly* 44(2): 350–383.

Schein, E. and Bennis, W. (1965) *Personal and Organizational Change via Group Methods*, New York: Wiley.

Isaacs, W. (1999) *Dialogue and the Art of Thinking Together*, New York: Doubleday.

Karpman, S. (1968) Fairy tales and script drama analysis, *Transactional Analysis Bulletin* 26(7): 39–43.

Abram, J. (2007) *The Language of Winnicott: A Dictionary of Winnicott's Use of Words*, London: Karnac.

Brown, B. (2015) *Daring Greatly: How the Courage to Be Vulnerable Transforms the Way We Live, Love, Parent, and Lead*, London: Penguin.

Choy, A. (1990) The Winner's Triangle, *Transactional Analysis Journal* 20(1): 40–46.

Berne, E. (1964) *Games People Play*, New York: Grove Press.

Stepper, J. (2020) *Working Out Loud: A 12-Week Method to Build New*

Connections, a Better Career, and a More Fulfilling Life, Edmonton: Ikigai Press.

Daloz, L. (1986) *Effective Teaching and Mentoring: Realizing the Transformational Power of Adult Learning Experiences*, San Francisco, CA: Jossey-Bass.

Blakey, J. and Day, I. (2012) *Challenging Coaching*, London: Nicholas Brealey Publishing.

Norman, C.E. (2020) *Mentor Coaching: A Practical Guide*, Maidenhead: Open University Press.

Pedrick, C. (2020) *Simplifying Coaching: How to Have More Transformational Conversations by Doing Less*, Maidenhead: Open University Press.

Edison, T. (1932) quoted in *Harper's Bazaar* magazine.

Quote Investigator (2014) Available at: https://quoteinvestigator.com/2014/05/22/solve, accessed: 30/3/2022.

ICF (2020) PCC Markers. Available at: https://coachingfederation.org/pcc-markers, accessed: 24/3/2022.

Eckstein, R. (1969) Concerning the teaching and learning of psychoanalysis, *Journal of the American Psychoanalytic Association* 17(2): 312–332.

Whitworth, L., Kimsey-House, H. and Sandahl, P. (1998) *Co-active Coaching*, Palo Alto, CA: Davies Black Publishing.

Harris, T. (1967) *I'm OK, you're OK*, New York: Grove Press.

Ernst, F. (1971) The OK Corral: the grid for get-on-with, *Transactional Analysis Journal* 1(4): 231–240.

Cameron, K. (2012) *Positive Leadership: Strategies for Extraordinary Performance*, Oakland, CA: Berrett-Koehler Publishers.

Mark, G., Gudith, D. and Klocke, U. (2008) The cost of interrupted work: More speed and stress, Conference on Human Factors in Computing Systems. Proceedings of the Conference on Human Factors in Computing Systems, ACM SIGCHI, Special Interest Group on Computer–Human Interaction, Florence, Italy, 5–10 April.

Markson, L. and Paterson, K.B. (2009) Effects of gaze-aversion on visual–spatial imagination, *British Journal of Psychology* 100(3): 553–563.

Oppezzo, M., and Schwartz, D.L. (2014) Give your ideas some legs: The positive effect of walking on creative thinking, *Journal of Experimental Psychology: Learning, Memory, and Cognition* 40(4): 1142–1152. Available at: www.apa.org/pubs/journals/releases/xlm-a0036577.pdf, accessed: 30/3/2022.

Argyris, C. (1990) *Overcoming Organizational Defences*, Needham, MA: Allyn & Bacon.

Covey, S. (1999) *The 7 Habits of Highly Effective People*, New York: Simon & Schuster.

Gallagher, K. (2020) *Lunar Living*, London: Yellow Kite.

Poynton, R. (2019) *Do/Pause: You Are Not Your To Do List*, London: The Do Book Company.

Agarwal, P.K. and Bain, P.M. (2019) *The Power of Teaching: Unleash the Science of Learning*, Hoboken, NJ: Wiley Publishing.

Chapter 2

Isaason, S. (2021) *How to Thrive as a Coach in a Digital World: Coaching with Technology*, Maidenhead, Open University Press

Broadwell, M.M. (1969) Teaching for learning, *The Gospel Guardian* 20(41): 1–3.

Amabile, T. and Kramer, S. (2011) *The Progress Principle: Using Small Wins to Ignite Joy, Engagement, and Creativity at Work*, Boston, MA: Harvard Business Review Press.

Gallwey, T. (2001) *The Inner Game of Work*, London: Random House.

Knowles, M. (1975). *Self-directed Learning*. Chicago: Follet.

Bird, J. and Gornall, S. (2015) *The Art of Coaching: A Handbook of Tips and Tools*, Abingdon: Routledge.

Pedrick, C. (2020) *Simplifying Coaching: How to Have More Transformational Conversations by Doing Less*, Maidenhead: Open University Press.

Rosenthal, R. and Jacobson, L. (1968) Pygmalion in the classroom. *The Urban Review* 3(1): 16–20.

Gabbard, G.O. (1982) The exit line: Heightened transference–countertransference manifestations at the end of the hour, *Journal of the American Psychoanalytic Association* 30(3): 579–598.

Blakey, J. and Day, I. (2012) *Challenging Coaching*, London: Nicholas Brealey Publishing.

Hawkins, P. and Smith, N. (2013) *Coaching, Mentoring and Organisational Consultancy, Supervision and Development*, 2nd edition, Maidenhead: Open University Press.

Franklin, M. (2019) *The Heart of Laser-Focused Coaching: A Revolutionary Approach to Masterful Coaching*, Wilmington: Thomas Noble Books.

Reynolds, M. (2020) *Coach the Person, Not the Problem: A Guide to Using Reflective Inquiry*, Oakland, CA: Berrett-Koehler Publishers.

Budd Rowe, M. (1972) Wait-time and rewards as instructional variables: Their influence on language, logic, and fate control, ERIC: https://eric.ed.gov/?id=ED061103.

Whitworth, L., Kimsey-House, H. and Sandahl, P. (1998) *Co-active Coaching*, Palo Alto, CA: Davies Black Publishing.

Dweck, C. (2017) *Mindset: Changing the Way You Think to Fulfil Your Potential*, 6th edition, London: Robinson.

Norman, C.E. (2020) *Mentor Coaching: A Practical Guide*, Maidenhead: Open University Press.

Berne, E. (1964) *Games People Play*, New York: Grove Press.

Morgan, K. (2019) *The Coach's Survival Guide*, Maidenhead: Open University Press.

Bion, W.R. (1967) Notes on memory and desire, *Psychoanalytic Forum* 2: 272–273.

Kahler, T. (1975) Drivers: The key to the process of scripts, *Transactional Analysis Journal* 5(3): 280–284.

Hay, J. (2009) *Transactional Analysis for Trainers*, 2nd edition, Hertford: Sherwood Publishing.

Klein, M. (1992) The enemies of love, *Transactional Analysis Journal* 22(2): 76–8.

Bridges, W. (2004) *Transitions: Making Sense of Life's Changes*, Boston, MA: Da Capo Press.

Chapter 3

Baumeister R.F. and Leary, M.R. (1995) The need to belong: Desire for interpersonal attachments as a fundamental human motivation, *Psychological Bulletin* 117: 497–529.

Bowlby, J. (1988) *A Secure Base: Parent–Child Attachment and Healthy Human Development*, New York: Basic Books.

Kahler, T. (1975) Drivers: The key to the process of scripts, *Transactional Analysis Journal* 5(3): 280–284.

Hay, J. (2009) *Transactional Analysis for Trainers*, 2nd edition, Hertford: Sherwood Publishing.

Blakey, J. and Day, I. (2012) *Challenging Coaching*, London: Nicholas Brealey Publishing.

Whittington, J. (2012) *Systemic Coaching and Constellations: An Introduction to the Principles, Practices and Application*, London: Kogan Page.

Ritchie, R. (1885) *Mrs. Dymond Smith*, London: Elder & Co.

Bridges, W. (2004) *Transitions: Making Sense of Life's Changes*, Boston, MA: Da Capo Press.

De Haan, E. and Sills, C. (2012) *Coaching Relationships: The Relational Coaching Field Book*, Farringdon: Libri Publishing.

Mental Health First Aid England (n.d.) Available at: https://mhfaengland.org, accessed: 30/3/2022.

Mental Health First Aid England (n.d.), Stress container. Available at: https://mhfaengland.org/mhfa-centre/resources/address-your-stress/whats-in-your-stress-container.mp4, accessed: 30/3/2022.

International Coaching Federation (ICF) (2019) Core competencies. Available at: https://coachfederation.org/core-competencies, accessed: 30/3/2022.

Williams Crenshaw, K. (1989) Demarginalizing the intersection of race and sex: A black feminist critique of antidiscrimination doctrine, feminist theory and antiracist politics, *University of Chicago Legal Forum* 140: 139–167.

Whitworth, L., Kimsey-House, H. and Sandahl, P. (1998) *Co-active Coaching*, Palo Alto, CA: Davies Black Publishing.

Carbado, D.W., Crenshaw, K.W., Mays, V.M. and Tomlinson, B. (2013) Intersectionality: Mapping the movements of a theory, *Du Bois Review: Social Science Research on Race* 10(2): 303–312.

Whitworth, L., Kimsey-House, H. and Sandahl, P. (1998) *Co-active Coaching*, Palo Alto, CA: Davies Black Publishing.

Greenstein, G. (2018) Power, privilege and oppression: An effective lens for executive coaching, Institute of Coaching. Available at: https://instituteofcoaching.org/blogs/power-privilege-and-oppression-effective-lens-executive-coaching, 13 February, accessed: 30/3/2022.

Chapter 4

Benjamin J. (2017) *Beyond Doer and Done to: An Intersubjective view of Thirdness*, Abingdon: Routledge.

Berne, E. (1964) *Games People Play*, New York: Grove Press.

Koroleva, N. (2016) A new model of sustainable change in executive coaching: Coachees' attitudes, required resources and routinisation, *International Journal of Evidence Based Coaching and Mentoring*, Special Issue 10: 84–97.

Karpman, S. (1968) Fairy tales and script drama analysis, *Transactional Analysis Bulletin* 26(7): 39–43.

Hawkins, P. and Smith, N. (2013) *Coaching, Mentoring and Organisational Consultancy, Supervision and Development*, 2nd edition, Maidenhead: Open University Press.

Bion, W.R. (1967) Notes on memory and desire, *Psychoanalytic Forum* 2: 272–273.

Kahler, T. (1975) Drivers: The key to the process of scripts, *Transactional Analysis Journal* 5(3): 280–284.

Bungay Stanier, M. (1996) The *Coaching Habit: Say Less, Ask More & Change the Way You Lead Forever*, Vancouver: Page Two.

Norman C. and Ridgley, S. (2021) The one exploring movement's relationship to learning, *Lifting the Lid*, podcast, ep. 55. Available at: https://podcasts.apple.com/gb/podcast/lifting-the-lid-episode-55-the-one-exploring/id1533533535?i=1000539038941 accessed: 30/3/2022.

Leary-Joyce, J. (2014) *The Fertile Void: Gestalt Coaching at Work*, London: AoEC Press.

Loukopoulos, L.D., Dismukes, R.K. and Barshi, I. (2009) *The Multitasking Myth: Handling Complexity in Real-world Operations*, London: Routledge.

Ward, A.F., Duke, K., Gneezy, A. and Bos, M.W. (2017) Brain drain: The mere presence of one's own smartphone reduces available cognitive capacity, *Journal of the Association for Consumer Research* 2(2): 140–154.

Amabile, T. and Kramer, S. (2011) *The Progress Principle: Using Small Wins to Ignite Joy, Engagement, and Creativity at Work*, Boston, MA: Harvard Business Review Press.

Franklin, M. (2019) *The HeART of Laser-focused Coaching: A Revolutionary Approach to Masterful Coaching*, Wilmington: Thomas Noble Books.

Reynolds, M. (2020) *Coach the Person, Not the Problem: A Guide to Using Reflective Inquiry*, Oakland, CA: Berrett-Koehler Publishers.

Chapter 5

Benjamin J. (2017) *Beyond Doer and Done to: An Intersubjective View of Thirdness*, Abingdon: Routledge.

Kline, N. (2002) *Time to Think*, London: Cassell.

Berne, E. (1964) *Games People Play*, New York: Grove Press.

Schiff, J.L., Mellor, K., Richman, D., Fishman, J., Wolz, L. and Mombe, D. (1975) *The Cathexis Reader: Transactional Analysis Treatment of Psychosis*, New York: Harper & Row.

International Coaching Federation (ICF) (2019) Coaching competencies. Available at: https://coachingfederation.org/core-competencies, accessed: 30/3/2022.

Francis Bacon (1597) Meditationes Sacrae. Available at: https://en.wikisource.org/wiki/Meditationes_sacrae?fbclid=I-wAR1_3LQm3b17sQHmjfWJgI2M0XnImg7SLcHzhKcecxzo_MisFfx-7GFkO1C0, accessed: 30/3/2022.

Janis, I.L. (1972) *Victims of Groupthink: A Psychological Study of Foreign-policy Decisions and Fiascos*, Boston, MA: Houghton Mifflin.

Baumeister R.F. and Leary M.R. (1995) The need to belong: Desire for interpersonal attachments as a fundamental human motivation, *Psychological Bulletin* 117: 497–529.

Bressler, M., Campbell, K. and Von Bergen, C.W. (2014) The Sandwich Feedback Method: Not very tasty, *Journal of Behavioral Studies in Business* 7: 1–16.

Brown, B. (2015) *Daring Greatly: How the Courage to Be Vulnerable Transforms the Way We Live, Love, Parent, and Lead*, London: Penguin.

Whitworth, L., Kimsey-House, H. and Sandahl, P. (1998) *Co-active Coaching*, Palo Alto, CA: Davies Black Publishing.

Rosenthal, R. and Jacobson, L. (1968) Pygmalion in the classroom. *The Urban Review* 3(1): 16–20.

Chapter 6

Whitworth, L., Kimsey-House, H. and Sandahl, P. (1998) *Co-active Coaching*, Palo Alto, CA: Davies Black Publishing.

Kolb, D.A. (1984) *Experiential Learning*, Englewood Cliffs, NJ: White Lotus Press.

Honey, P. and Mumford, A. (1986) *The Manual of Learning styles*, Maidenhead: Peter Honey Publications.

Hawkins, P. and Smith, N. (2011) Transformational coaching. In: Cox, E., Bachkirova, T. and Clutterbuck, D. (eds) *The Complete Handbook of Coaching*, London: Sage, pp. 231–246.

Norman, C.E. (1999) unpublished Master's dissertation on visualisation and its effects on change in behaviour, University of Leicester.

Whitmore, J. (2012) *Coaching for Performance: The Principles and Practice of Coaching and Leadership*, London: Nicholas Brealey Publishing.

Franklin, M. (2019) *The HeART of Laser-focused Coaching: A Revolutionary Approach to Masterful Coaching*, Wilmington: Thomas Noble Books.

Reynolds, M. (2020) *Coach the Person, Not the Problem: A Guide to Using Reflective Inquiry*, Oakland, CA, Berrett-Koehler Publishers.

Berry, R.M., Ashby, J.S., Gnilka, P.B. and Matheny, K.B. (2011) A comparison of face-to-face and distance coaching practices: Coaches' perceptions of the role of working alliance in problem resolution, *Consulting Psychology Journal: Practice and Research* 63(4): 243–253.

Markson, L. and Paterson, K.B. (2009) Effects of gaze-aversion on visual–spatial imagination, *British Journal of Psychology* 100(3): 553–563.

Kraus, M.W. (2017) Voice-only communication enhances empathic accuracy, *American Psychologist* 72(7): 644–654.

Froboese, I. (n.d.), Zentrum für Gesundheit at Sports University Cologne, original paper not found.

Ward, A.F., Duke, K., Gneezy, A. and Bos, M.W. (2017) Brain drain: The mere presence of one's own smartphone reduces available cognitive capacity, *Journal of the Association for Consumer Research* 2(2): 140–154.

Bandler, R. and Grinder, J. (1989) *The Structure of Magic: A Book About Language and Therapy*, vol. 1, Palo Alto, CA: Science and Behavior Books.

Di Pellegrino, G., Fadiga, L., Fogassi, L., Gallese, V. and Rizzolatti, G. (1992) Understanding motor events: A neurophysiological study. *Experimental Brain Research* 91: 176–180.

Hawkins, P. and Smith, N. (2013) *Coaching, Mentoring and Organisational Consultancy, Supervision and Development*, 2nd edition, Maidenhead: Open University Press.

Whitworth, L., Kimsey-House, H. and Sandahl, P. (1998) *Co-active Coaching*, Palo Alto, CA: Davies Black Publishing.

Berne, E. (1964) *Games People Play*, New York: Grove Press.

Chapter 7

Gardener, H. (2006[1983]) *Multiple Intelligences: New Horizons in Theory and Practice*, New York: Basic Books.

Dornhecker, M., Blake, J.J., Benden M., Zhao, H. and Wendel M. (2015) The effect of stand-biased desks on academic engagement: An exploratory study, *International Journal of Health Promotion and Education* 53(5): 271–280.

Oppezzo, M. and Schwartz, D.L. (2014) Give your ideas some legs: The positive effect of walking on creative thinking, *Journal of Experimental Psychology: Learning, Memory, and Cognition* 40(4): 1142–1152. Available at: www.apa.org/pubs/journals/releases/xlm-a0036577.pdf, accessed: 30/3/2022.

McGilchrist, I. (2019) *The Master and his Emissary, The Divided Brain and the Making of the Western World*, London: Perlego.

Armstrong, T. (2020) Multiple intelligences, American Institute for Learning and Human Development. Available at: www.institute4learning.com/resources/articles/multiple-intelligences, accessed: 30/3/2022.

Hawkins, P. and Turner, E. (2019) *Systemic Coaching: Delivering Value Beyond the Individual*, London: Routledge.

Rosenbaum, D., Mama, Y. and Algom, D. (2017) Stand by your stroop: Standing up enhances selective attention and cognitive control, *Psychological Science* 28(12): 1864–1867.

Hawkins, P. and Smith, N. (2013) *Coaching, Mentoring and*

Organisational Consultancy, Supervision and Development, 2nd edition, Maidenhead: Open University Press.

Luft, J. and Ingham, H. (1961) The Johari Window: A graphic model of awareness in interpersonal relations, *Human Relations Training News* 5(9): 6–7.

Amabile, T. and Kramer, S. (2011) *The Progress Principle: Using Small Wins to Ignite Joy, Engagement, and Creativity at Work*, Boston, MA: Harvard Business Review Press.

Whitworth, L., Kimsey-House, H. and Sandahl, P. (1998) Co-active Coaching, Palo Alto, CA: Davies Black Publishing.

Bridges, W. (2004) *Transitions: Making Sense of Life's Changes*, Boston, MA: Da Capo Press.

Karpman, S. (1968) Fairy tales and script drama analysis, *Transactional Analysis Bulletin* 26(7): 39–43.

Parkinson, C.N. (1955) *Parkinson's Law, Or the Pursuit of Progress*, London: John Murray.

Kahler, T. (1975) Drivers: The key to the process of scripts, *Transactional Analysis Journal* 5(3): 280–284.

Schiff, J.L., Mellor, K., Richman, D., Fishman, J., Wolz, L. and Mombe, D. (1975) *The Cathexis Reader: Transactional Analysis Treatment of Psychosis*, New York: Harper & Row.

Summary

Broadwell, M.M. (1969) Teaching for learning, *The Gospel Guardian* 20(41): 1–3.

Afterword

Norman, C.E. (2020) *Mentor Coaching: A Practical Guide*, Maidenhead: Open University Press.

Norman, C.E. (2018) Locked-in learning, *Coaching at Work* 13(6): 42–45.

Appendix 2

ICF (2019) PCC Markers. Available at: https://coachingfederation.org/pcc-markers, accessed: 31/3/2022.

Summary of the Shifts

Mindsets from... PARENTS & CARERS

OLD MINDSET	NEW MINDSET	PAGE
Do what I tell you to do	Provide psychological safety so the thinker can figure out their next move	2
Only children need boundaries	Adults need boundaries too	5
You should always try your hardest	This should be hard work for the thinker, not for the coach	7
It's rude to interrupt	It's useful to interrupt if it enables the thinker to move away from known thinking towards new thinking	15
Don't talk back	Challenge assumptions, offer disruptive reflections and insight into 'blind spots'	18
If you can't say something nice, don't say anything at all	Offer a ratio of 5.6:1 positive-to-constructive feedback	22
Mind your 'Ps and Qs'	Acknowledge who the thinker is being in the moment	24
Say 'sorry'	Let it be OK to make mistakes in a session	26
Eye contact is polite	Being side-by-side or audio-only allows for more vulnerability	28
Don't be nosy	Do be curious on the thinker's behalf	29
It's rude to look at the clock	We signal time checks to trigger new thinking	30
Don't get too big for your boots	Own your coaching strengths	32
Don't be selfish	Put your own oxygen mask on first	34

Mindsets from... SCHOOL

Mindsets from... PEERS

	OLD MINDSET	NEW MINDSET	PAGE
	Do what it takes to fit in	Be yourself	78
	Be likeable	Be challenging	80
	Think about a clever response before they stop talking	Don't think ahead; stay in the moment	82
	Here's what I would do	What is going to work for you given your personality and context?	84
	Breaking up is hard to do	Ending is necessary	86
	Let's do this...	How would it be if we did this...?	89
	Silence is awkward	Silence is golden thinking time	90
	The loudest voices have the most influence	Being there is useful in itself	92
	Don't air your dirty laundry in public	Ask about mental health	94
	We avoid discussions of difference	We acknowledge our own and others' unique privilege and restriction	96

Mindsets from... WORK

Mindsets from... MANAGERS

	OLD MINDSET	NEW MINDSET	PAGE
	You work for me	We work together	132
	The boss says jump, you say: 'how high?'	We talk about both our needs	134
	Come with solutions, not questions	Be OK with not knowing	136
	Knowledge is power	The coach's knowledge is limited	138
	Think like me	Challenge my assumptions	140
	I must have the answer when someone asks me a question	I can ask a question so the thinker finds their own answers	142
	Feedback is painful	Objective feedback is useful	144
	Why?	What and how?	146
	Always be professional	Show your human credentials	148
	People are not resourceful	People can figure it out with support	150
	Lead them to the answers that are 'good for them'	Only the thinkers know what is good for them	151
	I need to produce and send written notes	Thinkers are adults and can capture their learning in words that are true to them	153

Mindsets from... COACH TRAINING

Mindsets from... COACHING EXPERIENCE

	OLD MINDSET	NEW MINDSET	PAGE
	We sit and talk	We use all the thinker's senses to access new learning	180
	Start from the end of the last session	They are now a different person	182
	Work on the presenting problem	The presenting problem is rarely the problem	183
	Coach the individual	Coach the system	185
	Building trust takes time	Cut to the chase	188
	There are lists of powerful questions	Powerful questions lose their potency in any other coaching conversation	190
	Build psychometric tests, 360-degree feedback or personality assessments into the start of a coaching programme	Assessments set up a Parent-Child rather than an Adult-Adult relationship	192
	When a session is over, it's over	Closing the session fully allows for continued new thinking afterwards	194
	Coaching sessions are a set length	It's OK to finish early	196
	There is scarcity of time, resources and people	Adopt an abundance mentality	198
	Keep calm and carry on	Take recovery time before you need it	200
	Pride comes before a fall	Account for your whole self, and enable thinkers to account for their whole self	202

I hope this index is useful to you as you continue to unlearn what you have learned, in pursuit of that illusive coaching mastery. Keep coming back to it, as mastery is a perpetual process.

About the author

I've made no secret of my mission to professionalise the coaching industry. I contend that both mentor coaching and supervision should be mandated by professional coaching bodies as part of coaches' continuing professional development.

With over 20 years of coaching experience, Clare Norman is highly sought after by other expert coaches, as well as successful coach training companies as a Master Mentor Coach.

Clare looks to continually sharpen individuals' coaching edge and upskill mentor coaches so they can deliver high-quality feedback to their coaches-in-development. Her laser focus on mindset shifts and her knack for spotting marginal gains has made her a go-to person for coaches looking for mentorship and practical, meaningful ways to improve their practice.

With an international following from both her coaching peers and senior leadership, Clare is making a difference to the world of work via the professional application of coaching.

Her mission across all her work is to encourage leaders to put people and the planet before profits. In 2015, Clare started her own business, Clare Norman Coaching Associates. Drawing on 25 years of learning and development experience gleaned from leading L&D strategy within NatWest and Accenture, she specialises in transition and leadership coaching, alongside mentor coaching and coaching supervision.

Clare's first book, *Mentor Coaching: A Practical Guide*, is a work of passion and according to Fran Fisher MCC, 'makes a significant contribution to the conscious evolution of the coaching profession, [and] offers a new paradigm for coach mentoring and the continuous personal and professional development of the coach.'

Living in the New Forest, Hampshire with her bloodhound and husband, Clare is a prolific blogger and an award-winning regular feature writer for industry magazines and journals. She is also a popular speaker, often called upon to deliver webinars and keynotes to fellow coaches looking to sharpen their edge.